Mother Ross

Mother Ross

The Life and Adventures of Mrs. Christian Davies,
Commonly Called Mother Ross on Campaign
with the Duke of Marlborough

Daniel Defoe

LEONAUR

Mother Ross
The Life and Adventures of Mrs. Christian Davies, Commonly Called Mother Ross
on Campaign with the Duke of Marlborough
by Daniel Defoe

First published under the title
The Life and Adventures of Mrs. Christian Davies, Commonly Called Mother Ross

Leonaur is an imprint of Oakpast Ltd

Copyright in this form © 2011 Oakpast Ltd

ISBN: 978-0-85706-717-3 (hardcover)
ISBN: 978-0-85706-718-0 (softcover)

http://www.leonaur.com

Publisher's Notes

Contents

Preface

In the following life of Mrs. Christian Davies, taken from her own mouth, we may remark examples of uncommon intrepidity but rarely found in the fair sex. By her having been long conversant in the camp, she had lost that softness which heightens the beauty of the fair, and contracted a masculine air and behaviour, which however excusable in her, would hardly be so in any other of her sex.

She was long before her death afflicted with a complication of distempers, as dropsy, scurvy, &c., at length her husband being taken ill, she would sit up with him at nights, by which she contracted a cold that threw her into a continual fever, which carried her off in four days.

She died on the 7th of July, 1739, and was interred in the burying-ground belonging to Chelsea Hospital, with military honours.

Her Life and Entertaining Adventures

I was born in Dublin, in the year 1667, of parents whose probity acquired them that respect from their acquaintance, which they had no claim to from their birth. My father was both a malster and brewer; in which business he employed at least twenty servants, beside those under the direction of my mother, in a farm he hired of Arthur White, of Leslip, esq.; left entirely to her care. My father was remarkable for industry and vigilance in his affairs, which employing his whole time in town, he never saw my mother but on Sundays, except some extraordinary business required his visiting the farm, which, though of fourscore pounds a year, she managed with great prudence and economy.

They were both very tender of me, and spared no cost in my education, though I did not make the best use of their care in this article I had patience, indeed, to learn to read, and become a good needle-woman, but I had too much mercury in me to like a sedentary life, the reason that I was always at the farm to assist my mother; this I did as much through inclination as duty, being delighted with a country life, it indulging to my love of ramping, and the pleasure I took in manly employments; for I was never better pleased than when I was following the plough, or had a rake, flail, or pitchfork in my hand, which implements I could handle with as much strength and dexterity, if not with more, than any of my mother's servants.

I used to get astride upon the horses, and ride them bare-backed about the fields, leaped hedges and ditches, by which I once got a terrible fall, and spoiled a grey mare given to my brother by our grandfather. My father never knew how this mischief happened, which brought me under contribution to a cowherd, who saw me tumble the mare into a dry ditch, and whose secrecy I was obliged to purchase, by giving him, for a considerable time, a cup of ale every night, I shall pass by the wild girlish tricks I and my companions were constantly playing, as they can administer nothing entertaining, and mention one only, to show an odd curiosity in a nobleman.

I and four of my companions, were rolling ourselves down a hill, and turning heels over head, when the Earl of C——d was passing in his coach, drawn by six beautiful grey horses, by the road, divided from the scene of our diversion by a quickset hedge and a ditch. He stopped his coach to be a spectator of our gambols; but finding that we put an end to our pastime on our perceiving him, (for the youngest of us was seventeen, and consequently had sense enough to think the showing our naked tails not over-decent,) he called to us, and promising to give us a crown apiece, if we would begin and pursue our diversion; our modesty gave way to our avarice, we indulged his lordship's optics, and he, having been amply satisfied by the unreservedness of our performance, kept his word.

I said that I was as active and strong in all the labours of husbandry, as any of our servants; I will therefore give one instance of this. About the beginning of August, 1685, I was employed to stack wheat, and was on the top of one near fifty-four foot high, when I perceived in the road near our farm, the judges and other magistrates in their robes, preceded by kettle-drums, trumpets, and heralds, in their rich coats, coming up the hill, in order to proclaim King James. Animated by the martial music, and desirous to have a nearer view of this glorious sight, which, with the glare of the gold and silver coats, the heralds, trumpets, and kettle-drums wore, had, in a manner, dazzled my sight, I leaped down, ran to, and cleared with a leap a five-barred gate, which was between me and the road they passed, calling to my mother to come and see the show, as I imagined every man there at least a prince. My mother hearing the procession was to proclaim King James, went back, and wept bitterly for some time, but would never tell me the reason for her tears.

Nothing remarkable occurs to my memory from the time of this monarch's being proclaimed, to that in which he was forced to throw himself into the arms of his Irish subjects, having been driven from the throne of England by King William. The Irish very readily espoused his cause, and among others (from a consciousness of its being a duty incumbent on him to support his lawful sovereign, notwithstanding his being of a different religion, which he thought not reason sufficient to affect his loyalty) my father sold all his standing corn, and other things of value, to Mr. Ascham, a neighbouring farmer, and was thus enabled, with what ready money he had by him before, to raise a troop of horse, and provide them with accoutrements, and everything necessary to take the field; and having furnished himself with a fine horse, and whatever else was requisite, he set out at the head of this troop, which was called by his name, Cavenaugh's, to join the rest of the army.

I remember I was very fond of riding this horse, for a reason which would have prevented any other of my sex venturing upon him; I mean his mettle; for he was so fiery, that not one of the troop durst mount him. You will, perhaps, wonder how I could; but I had so often fed him with bread and oats, that he would stand for me to take him up, when at grass, though he would have given twenty men work enough to catch him. When I had once hold of him, I would put on his bridle and lead him into a ditch and bestride him bare-backed. I have often mounted him when saddled, and took great pleasure to draw and snap the pistols, and have not seldom made my friends apprehend for my life. I mention this, not as worth notice, but only to show my inclinations, while a girl, were always masculine.

My father having sold his corn standing, as I have already observed, without my mother's knowledge, occasioned a quarrel, in which some of Mr. Ascham's and our men were wounded. After my father was gone to the army, my mother sent reapers into the field to cut the corn; these met with others, sent by the then proprietor, upon the same errand. Words immediately arose, and they very soon came to blows, making use of their sickles, a desperate weapon. The noise soon reached my mother's ears, who understanding how the matter was, withdrew her troops; but not without some difficulty, and having regaled them in her house with a good breakfast and strong liquors, they were at length appeased and dismissed.

While my father bore arms for King James, the neighbouring papists, in time of divine service, came to, and blocked up the church door of Leslip, with butchers' blocks, and other lumber. My mother was then in the church; I was at home, but hearing the noise, and fearing my mother might receive some hurt, I snatched up a spit, and, thus armed, sallied forth to force my way, and come to her assistance; but being resisted by a sergeant, I thrust my spit through the calf of his leg, removed the things which had blocked up the door, and called to my mother, bidding her come away, for dinner was ready. In the

11

scuffle, the Reverend Mr. Malary, the clerk, with several others, were wounded, and I taken into custody for having hurt the sergeant; but upon being heard, and representing the hardship of being interrupted in our worship, when my father was actually in arms for the service of the prince for whom they pretended great zeal, though in fact, they ought rather to be esteemed his concealed enemies, since, by such actions, they alienated the hearts of his subjects, and gave ground to his enemies to raise a clamour, I was acquitted.

The Battle of the Boyne put an end to all my father's hopes for King James; for his army was there defeated, and he, with the rest of the shattered troops, trusted their safety to the swiftness of their horses' heels, rather than to the strength of their own arms. My father, in company with a very handsome young French gentleman, who served as lieutenant in the king's forces, made the best of his way to our house, without staying to bait on the road. My mother, who understood what belonged to good manners, as she had been genteelly educated by her father, Bryan Bembrick, of Wheatly, in the bishopric of Durham, esq.; who had a particular care to bring up his children in a polite manner, received the stranger with great civility, and having ordered them a hot supper, prepared my bed for his reception that night; but he lay no longer than till three of the morning, when my father, alarmed with the noise of some of his friends who fled from the conquerors, imagining they were the victorious forces of King William, in pursuit of the defeated remains of King James's army, roused the French officer, and got out their horses with the utmost expedition.

While they were saddling, my father took a short, but sorrowful leave of his wife and children, whom, with tears in his eyes, he blessed and recommended to the Divine protection: then turning to my mother, 'My dear,' said he, 'do not be dejected; comfort yourself, that whatever misfortunes befall us, we suffer in a just cause, and for having done what is the duty of every loyal subject; at least, my conscience tells me, that I have acted as I ought, and as I was bound to do by my oath of allegiance, from which I know no power on earth that can absolve me. *The Lord giveth, and the Lord taketh away, blessed be the name of the Lord,* His ways are inscrutable, and I humbly submit to his decrees, which are all founded in wisdom. As for you, keep at home with your children, and be their support, for you being a protestant, need apprehend no danger from the enemy; may they hereafter repay your maternal care and tenderness by a filial duty, and prove your comfort;

but never torment yourself with uneasy thoughts for your unfortunate husband. Think of me no more.'

'God forbid,' said she, and bursting into a flood of tears; my father, who could not bear to see her weep, as he loved her with a sincere tenderness, ran out of the room, and he and the officer mounting their horses, fled with precipitation. My mother was in too great affliction to admit of any rest, and rose immediately; but we, who did not take my father's departure so much to heart, lay till daybreak.

About twelve months after this, we had news of King James's forces, commanded by Monsieur St. Ruth, being defeated at the Battle of Aghrim, where General Ginkle obtained a complete victory. In this battle my father was dangerously wounded; though, by the skill of able surgeons, who attended him, he was in a fair way of recovery; but the night before he intended to return to his family, one Kelly, an Irish papist, who served him, taking the advantage of his hurt, and of a dark night, ran away with his horses to General Ginkle's army. This villainous ingratitude from a man whom he had always treated with great humanity, had such an effect on my father, that he was seized with a fever, which carried him off in a short time.

After the battle, in which the French general St. Ruth was killed, the English laid siege to Limerick. Captain Bodeaux, who, after the battle of the Boyne, fled with my father to our house, was here in garrison, and commanded that body of troops which defended the bridge, in which post he behaved with so much gallantry, that he was admired, and his death lamented, by even his enemies, who, to their great surprise, found, on stripping this brave officer, that it was a woman had given such proof of an invincible courage.

Though my mother had, during my father's illness, procured him a pardon for having appeared in arms, and levied men for the service of King James, yet, notwithstanding, the government seized upon all his effects.

I had, by this time, attained to an age of maturity, and happening to take the eye of a son of my mother's first cousin, named Thomas Howel, whose uncle, on the father's side, was a bishop, himself a student, and fellow of Dublin college, he made warm love to me; and for two years together carried on his addresses: his assiduity, and the opinion I had of his sincerity, were not without effect in his favour; and such that I found my esteem for him greater than my concern for my own interest; for having no fortune to bring him, except a barrel of brass crowns, which King James was not in a condition to pay in silver, I would not consent to his ruin; though he might, as he proposed, support us, by keeping a Latin school. When we eagerly wish a thing, we seldom examine thoroughly the consequences which may attend the possession of what we desire; and, if we cannot help seeing the evils probably consequential of the completion of our wishes, we easily satisfy ourselves with arguments which flatter our inclinations, however weak: this was his case; for when I laid before him the certain poverty which would attend his marrying a woman without a fortune, he removed the objection, at least as to his own part, with the airy prospect of preferments in the church; and in the interim, with what money he could get by a school, sufficient, as he flattered himself, to maintain me like a lady: and when I represented to him the deplorable condition of a clergyman's widow, with, possibly, a number of children; he answered, that his economy should ward against that evil. I, who looked upon all this as a castle in the air, would not consent to what he wished and thought, his happiness, though I could not esteem it other than his undoings as well as my own ruin; and therefore very seriously begged of him to give over his pursuits, but to no purpose: he still continued his visits and solicitations, which were more frequent, longer, and more urgent than usual.

One day he came to see me when I was the only person in the house, and then busied in making the beds; he laid hold of the opportunity, threw himself at my feet, embraced my knees, and urged his suit with such vehemence, such warmth of expression, such tender embraces, such ardent kisses, that finding by my eyes, and short breath, I had catched the contagious desire, he added force to vows of eternal constancy and marriage, and, with little resistance on my side, throwing me upon the bed, deprived me of that inestimable jewel which a maiden ought to preserve preferable to life. He stayed not long after his having perpetrated a deed which gave me up a prey to the deepest melancholy; when, on his withdrawing, he gave room for bitter reflection. I repented my weakness; and, with sincere tears of penitence, cursed the time, myself, and the undoer; I raved, tore my hair, and was not far from madness.

My mother and the rest of the family stayed abroad till evening; and my reason returning, I endeavoured to compose myself that I might not betray my folly: my eyes being pretty much swollen, my mother took notice of it, and asked me what was the matter; but she received only an evasive answer. I could get no rest all the following night, and the remembrance of what had passed, had such an effect upon me that I lost both my colour and stomach; I hated to see any of my acquaintance, and would, if possible, have hid me from the light of the sun: my melancholy was such, that every one took notice of it, and my afflicted mother, sensibly touched with this sudden change, often tenderly inquired of me what ground I had for the sadness which gave her so much uneasiness; for she feared so sudden and settled a grief, as was impossible for me to dissemble, would endanger my life.

She could draw nothing from me, but a request to quit her house; which she readily agreeing to, in hopes a change of air and company might produce also a change in my temper, sent me to my aunt's, who kept a public house in Dublin. Here I often met my student, but so carefully avoided allowing him any opportunity of speaking to me, and took such an inveterate hatred to him, that he at last was sensible his pursuit was vain. My melancholy, after I found no ill-consequence attend our guilt, began to wear off by degrees, and I gradually recovered my colour and cheerfulness of temper. I lived with my aunt upwards of four years, and behaved to her with such dutiful respect, such observance and vigilance, and with such a reserved, yet obliging manner to others, that I entirely captivated her good opinion, and engaged her tenderness; for, at her death, she left me sole heiress to all she had, and in possession of a house well-furnished, and well-accustomed.

I now received the reward of my prudent behaviour; I lived in ease and plenty; my business was considerable; I got money apace, and was esteemed by all my neighbours and acquaintance. Never woman was in a happier situation; for I was at the height of my ambition, and had not a wish to make. In a word, I was thoroughly content, and had reason so to be, till love, too often the bane of our sex; love, who has not seldom ruined noble families, nay, destroyed cities, and lain kingdoms waste; envious of the calm I enjoyed, came to imbitter my peace, disturb the tranquillity of my life, and make me know, by experience, the short duration of all sublunary satisfaction. Richard Welsh, a young fellow who had served my aunt, and, after her death, continued in the same capacity with me, found the way to my heart. He was very well made in his person, had a handsome, manly face; was of a generous, open temper; sober, vigilant, and active in his business; very regular in his life, and modest in his behaviour.

In a word, he was, or appeared to me, a man whom any woman might love without having her good sense called in question. My pride, at first, made me endeavour to stifle this growing passion, and I tried to conquer it by reason. I thought it would be a reflection upon

15

me to marry my servant, and I was sensible that it must be to the disadvantage of my fortune; for though by his economy he had saved some money, yet was it a trifle to what my aunt left me, and which my business was still daily improving: but love and reason seldom agree, and when once that despotic tyrant gets possession of the heart, he will also rule the head: my pride and reason made but vain efforts, and he would listen to neither; the more they disputed, the more absolute the little domineerer grew; in a very little time he humbled my haughtiness, and silenced my reason: the sight of Richard Welsh overturned the strongest resolutions that I could make; his name was music to my ears; if I did not see him, no other object could please my eyes, and I knew no other happiness but in possession of Richard Welsh.

Though my pride and reason were thoroughly vanquished, yet my modesty held out; for I thought it indecent, and a reflection on my sex, to make the first overture. This caused me many a restless night, till I thought on an expedient, which was to acquaint one of my friends with my situation, and engage her to put Richard upon making his addresses to me. She found an opportunity of talking to him in private, which she did in the following manner.

'Richard, I have thought your mistress happy in so trusty and sprightly a servant, who so well understands, and takes such honest care of her business; I know she is very sensible of your deserts, and gives you an excellent character; nay, I have heard her talk of you in such a manner, that between you and me, friend Richard, I fancy she has a sneaking kindness for you, and I believe it would be no hard matter for you to carry her, and be master instead of servant in the house, if you have the courage to make the attack. As I fancy I am not much out in my conjecture, I was resolved to take the first opportunity to acquaint you with your good fortune, if I am not deceived, as I believe I am not; make the best of this advice, and remember the proverb. *Faint heart never won fair lady.*'

Richard answered, that he liked his mistress very well, and he had a very good place, which he should be loath to lose, as he was afraid he should, if he made such an attempt, and did not succeed.

'Believe me, Richard,' said my friend, 'none of us all are displeased at being admired; we may pretend to be angry; but it is but a cloak to cover the inward satisfaction we find in being capable to inspire love. Your mistress is a woman, young, and not exempt from the failings of her sex: try your fortune with her, and, my life on it, you carry her.'

Richard thanked her, and promised he would follow her advice, which he did, in such terms as still endeared him more to me. I made, at first, some difficulty to hear him out; and putting on an air of severity, which, however, he might plainly perceive was counterfeit, bid him mind the business of the house as he ought to do, and he would find a cure for his pretended passion, which was the common effect of idleness. Richard catched at the words pretended and idleness.

'My dear mistress,' said he, 'if your modesty would allow you to view yourself with the same impartiality as others look upon you, your glass would convince you, that nobody is more capable to give love, and consequently mine is not pretended, or the effect of idleness, since your own approbation of my diligence frees me from that imputation. No, I love you sincerely; and it is the effect of your agreeable temper. If I have not sooner told you this, it was my fear of displeasing you, and losing my place; for I find so great a pleasure in being near, and seeing you, that I prefer that alone to all the profit, were it ten times as much, of your service; and will rather continue your servant, than accept of being master of the best-accustomed house in Dublin, to lose the satisfaction which I find in the sight of you.'

'Very romantic truly,' said I; 'no doubt you have been studying some book of compliments, and come to practise upon me.'

'There needs no study,' replied Richard, 'to speak the sentiments of my heart; and though your modesty dissembles it, I am certain you must be conscious that it can be no easy matter to see, and converse with you, as I have done, and not be sensible of the effects of so many allurements.'

'Away to your business,' cried I; 'I don't love flattery; and I know too well the character of your sex, to believe a word any one of you utter; for your dissimulation goes hand-in-hand with your profession; I will hear no more; begone, I say, and think you are well off that I don't show more anger, which your former diligence prevents.'

'You can't', answered he, 'be more severe in your punishment of my faults, than to banish me thus without the least glimpse of hopes.'

'Go, go,' said I, 'repent this impertinence, and, if you can find a plausible excuse, I will give you a hearing at night when the company is gone.'

'O, let me thank you,' cried my saucy rogue, 'for this goodness;' and seizing me in his arms, he almost stifled me with kisses. I never before was so well pleased, though I pretended to be terrible angry, and threatened, if ever he was rude again, I would make him repent it.

'Faith, my dear mistress,' replied he, 'you have given me such a taste of happiness, that I will undergo any punishment to repeat it;' as he indeed instantly did, and I was better pleased, and more angry, and bid him get out of my sight, and attend the customers; which, being called upon, he did, not at all frightened with my threats.

I went soon after into my bar, where Richard watched my looks, and finding I turned away my head and blushed when I met his eyes, he interpreted it a good omen, and resolved to push his point. At night, when the company was all gone, notwithstanding my resentment of Richard's rudeness, he had the impudence to come into my chamber, telling the maid he was going to settle some accounts with me. As soon as I saw him, I asked him if he had forgot his late rudeness; for, if he had not, he showed an uncommon assurance, in daring to come into my sight. He replied, he was a servant, and as he had always obeyed my orders, he should be now wanting to his duty, if he had not come; and that he was resolved never to be, while he had the pleasure of being under my roof. I desired to know what he meant.

'You gave me order,' said he, 'to come and excuse myself for a fault which I own I can't repent.'

'O,' said I, 'I will rather forgive you without hearing your excuse, than expose myself to the like impertinence.'

'Indeed, my dear mistress, till you are less inviting, I am of opinion, I shall never be cured of my impertinence, though you may, if you please, change that word, and call it, as it really is, a sincere, disinterested fondness, by making your man your husband. I will be still your servant; and, as I have always studied your interest, I shall then study both that, and your happiness; your ease shall be my constant care; and you shall continue as much mistress of what you have, and dispose of it as you now do: for I shall never know any pleasure but that of pleasing you.'

I answered, that if he could persuade me to believe him, the world must censure me very much to marry my servant, a man without a fortune, when I had enough, and was in a way of business to live easy. To this he answered, that our happiness did not depend on the opinion of the world; for do what we will, we cannot please everybody; that it was more reasonable for me to imagine, I should be happy with a man that loved me, even to doating, and whom I had also engaged by a tie of gratitude, than with one whom I married with a view of interest. That a great many rich people were strangers to that ease and content, which they had reason to envy in many much beneath them in fortune. That for his part, he should slight the censure of the world, were he the master, and I the servant, and, consulting only his own happiness, look upon what he possessed, no further valuable than as it would prove the sincerity of his love, by making me mistress of it all.

He then threw himself on his knees, and grasping mine in a sort of ecstasy, he continued; 'Believe me, my dear mistress, I have no view of interest; I love you for yourself, not for your money; of which I will never pretend to be other than a just steward, would you consent to make me the happiest man alive.'

I bid him get up, and as it was late, leave me to go to bed, and I would consider on what he had said. He answered. That I could not expect he could obey such cruel orders without some consideration. 'Suffer me to take one kiss, that I may flatter myself I have recovered your favour, and you shall see me all obedience.'

'Well, well,' said I, 'anything to get rid of you.'

On this, he snatched me in his arms, kissed and embraced me with an ardour that almost took away my senses, as well as my breath, and left my room: he had put me into such an agitation, and I fetched my breath so short and thick, that when I had a little recovered myself, I trembled at the risk I had run, and attributed my not being again surprised, rather to his respect, which prevented the attempt, than to any power I should have had to resist him.

This reflection made me resolve not to admit him any more into my chamber till he had a right to do what he pleased, and it would be my duty not to resist him. To be short, he continued his solicitations, and my friend who had put him upon them, pretended to plead on his behalf; I seemed to yield to the strength of her reasons, and we were married in a week after the first declaration. I expected to be censured by all my acquaintance for having married my servant; but I was agreeably disappointed, and they, on the contrary, complimented me upon the prudence of my choice.

Richard proved a tender, careful, and obliging husband; and as he promised, left me as much mistress of my effects, as I was when single. Whatever I did was well done, and he never seemed so well pleased, as when he had an opportunity to please me. He neither altered his dress, nor his manner of life; while he was servant he was always tight and clean, which, by the vails he got, besides his wages, he might very well be. When he was master, he bought neither more suits, nor finer cloth; his change of fortune, made no change in his temper or behaviour; he was altogether as fearful of giving me the least cause of complaint; was humble to our customers, and, if possible, more active and vigilant in our business. He never forgot himself; and if sometimes gentlemen made him sit down with them, he paid them the same deference, and did not saucily, like too many publicans, imagine their condescension set him upon a foot with them, and gave him a license to talk and behave impertinently.

He was remarkable for his sobriety, which, with his modesty, good sense, and entertaining wit, endeared him to the best company that frequented the house. In a word, he had good sense, which he made a proper use of, and never would drown. We lived happily four years without any intervening misfortune; in which time, I brought him two fine boys, and was big of my third child, when the fickle goddess, weary of lavishing on me her favours, turned her back upon me, and resolved to make me sensible that she deserved the epithet of variable.

Alderman Forest, in James-street, furnished us with beer, and my husband went one day thither to pay him 50*l*,; but, to my great surprise, and contrary to custom, he did not return all that day: this gave me some uneasiness, which increased when it was grown entirely dark; but when the night advanced, and I heard no news of him, I concluded he must of necessity be murdered, for the sake of the money he had carried out, and grew quite outrageous. I despatched people every way to find him, but all their endeavours were to no manner of purpose; they heard, indeed, that he had been at the alderman's, and he owned the receipt of the money, but could give no account of him; other than that a gentleman was in his company when he paid the 50*l*., and that they went away together. I now concluded, (though, as it proved, very unjustly,) that the person mentioned to have been with him, had, upon some private pique, murdered him, and conveyed away his body.

My grief for his loss, for all search proved vain, was equal to the tender affection I bore him, and made me unfit to look after my house; the care of which I trusted to a nominal friend, who I found took care of her own interest to the prejudice of mine; for, instead of gaining while she had the management of my affairs, I ran out money.

Time having somewhat mollified my grief, and a twelvemonth having elapsed since my husband had disappeared, I bought mourning for myself and children, and took upon me the care of the business.

After having given my dear Richard over for dead, I was surprised by the receipt of a letter from him, which was as follows:

Dear Cristian,

This is the twelfth letter I have sent you without any answer to my former, which would both surprise and very much grieve me, did I not flatter myself that your silence proceeds from the miscarriage of my letters. It is from this opinion that I repeat the account of my sudden and unpremeditated departure, and the reason of my having enlisted for a soldier. It was my misfortune, when I went out to pay the alderman the 50*l.*, to meet Ensign C——m, who having formerly been my schoolfellow, would accompany me to the alderman's house, from whence we went, at his request, and took a hearty bottle at the tavern, where he paid the reckoning; having got a little too much wine in my head, I was easily persuaded to go on board a vessel that carried recruits, and take a bowl of punch, which I did in the captain's cabin, where being pretty much intoxicated, I was not sensible of what was doing upon deck. In the interim, the wind sprang up fair, the captain set sail with what recruits were on board, and we had so quick a passage, that we reached Helvoet Sluys before I had recovered from the effects of liquor.

It is impossible for me to paint the despair I was in, finding myself thus divided from my dear wife and children, landed on a strange shore, without money or friends to support me. I raved, tore my hair, and curst my drunken folly, which had brought upon me this terrible misfortune, which I thought in vain to remedy by getting a ship to carry me back, but there was none to be found.

The ensign, who possibly did not intend me this injury, did all he could to comfort me, and advised me to make a virtue of necessity, and take on in some regiment. My being destitute and unknown, compelled me to follow his advice, though with the greatest reluctance, and I now am, though much against my inclination, a private sentinel in Lord O——y's regiment of foot, where I fear I must pass the remainder of a wretched life, under the deepest affliction for my being deprived of the comfort I enjoyed while blessed with you and my dear babies: if Providence, in his mercy, does not relieve me; the hopes of which, and of once embracing those alone who engross my tenderest affection, you, my dearest Christian, and my poor children, make me endeavour to support my misfortune, and preserve a life, which, without you, would he too miserable to be worth

the care of your
Unfortunate, but ever loving husband,
Richard Welsh.

This letter renewed my grief, and gave new fountains to my eyes. I had bewailed him dead, and now I lamented him living, looking upon his unfortunate situation worse than death, as he was deprived of all means of returning to me; for I despaired of his officers parting with him. When I had read the letter, I was at first stupefied; I stood without motion, and my trouble being too great to allow of tears, I gave a sudden shriek and fell down, without the least signs of life remaining in me. When, by the care and charity of my friends and neighbours who came to my assistance, I was brought to my senses and speech, I burst into a flood of tears; but when I was asked the occasion of this sudden grief, I, for some time, answered nothing, but. 'My dear Richard, O must I never see thee more! O my dear, dear husband! once the comfort of my life, now the source of my misfortunes, I can never support the loss.'

In a word, I was in such agonies, and fainted so often, that they who were about me almost despaired of my life, or if I survived this new affliction, of which I was not capable to give them an account, that it would be the loss of my senses. Some of my friends would watch with me that night, and had it not been for their care, I had certainly put an end to that life which I thought insupportable. In the getting me to bed, my letter dropped, and their curiosity having taught them the cause of my distracting trouble, they endeavoured to comfort me with the hopes of recovering my husband; but to no purpose, I was inconsolable, and closed not my eyes all that night; in the morning I thought of going in search of my dear Richard, and this gave some ease to my tortured mind.

I began to flatter myself that I should meet no great difficulty in finding him out, and resolved in one of his suits, for we were both of a size, to conceal my sex, and go directly for Flanders, in search of him whom I preferred to everything else the world could afford me, which, indeed, had nothing alluring, in comparison with my dear Richard, and whom the hopes of seeing had lessened every danger to which I was going to expose myself. The pleasure I found in the thoughts of once more regaining him, recalled my strength, and I was grown much gayer than I had been at any time in my supposed widowhood. I was not long deliberating, after this thought had possessed me, but immediately set about preparing what was necessary for my ramble; and disposing of my children, my eldest with my mother, and that which was born after my husband's departure, with a nurse, (my second son was dead,) I told my friends, that I would go to England in search of my husband, and return with all possible expedition after I had found him.

My goods I left in the hands of such friends as had spare house-room, and my house I let to a cooper. Having thus ordered my affairs, I cut off my hair, and dressed me in a suit of my husband's, having had the precaution to quilt the waistcoat, to preserve my breasts from hurt, which were not large enough to betray my sex, and putting on the wig and hat I had prepared, I went out and bought me a silver-hilted sword, and some Holland shirts: but was at a loss how I should carry my money with me, as it was contrary to law to export above 5*l* out of the kingdom; I thought at last of quilting it in the waistband of my breeches, and by this method I carried with me fifty guineas without suspicion.

I had now nothing upon my hands to prevent my setting out; wherefore, that I might get as soon as possible to Holland, I went to the sign of the Golden Last, where Ensign Herbert Laurence, who was beating up for recruits, kept his rendezvous. He was in the house at the time I got there, and I offered him my service to go against the French, being desirous to show my zeal for His Majesty King William, and my country. The hopes of soon meeting with my husband, added a sprightliness to my looks, which made the officer say, I was a clever brisk young fellow; and having recommended my zeal, he gave me a guinea enlisting money, and a crown to drink the king's health, and ordered me to be enrolled, having told him my name was Christopher Welsh, in Captain Tichbourn's company of foot, in the regiment commanded by the Marquis de Pisare. The lieutenant of our company was Mr. Gardiner, our ensign Mr. Welsh.

We stayed but a short time in Dublin after this, but, with the rest of the recruits, were shipped for Holland, weighed anchor, and soon arrived at Williamstadt, where we landed and marched to Gorcum. Here our regimentals and first mountings were given us. The next day we set out for Gertrudenburg, and proceeded forward to Landen, where we were incorporated in our respective regiments, and then joined the grand army, which was in expectation of a general battle, the enemy being very near within cannon-shot. Having been accustomed to soldiers, when a girl, and delighted with seeing them exercise, I very soon was perfect, and applauded by my officers for my dexterity in going through it.

In a day or two after we arrived at Landen, I was ordered on the night guard, and, by direction of my officer, was posted at the bed-chamber door of the elector of Hanover. Mustapha, a Turk, and *valet-de-chambre* to his most serene highness, while I was here upon duty, introduced to the elector, a fine, handsome, jolly lady, who was what we call a black beauty; she was dressed in a rich silk, and her gown was tied with ribbons from her breast to her feet. I thought the lady went with a great deal of alacrity, as I believe many more of our sex would visit a sovereign prince with a particular satisfaction; especially if agreeable in his person, as the elector, who then wore his own hair, and the finest I ever saw, really was. When I saw His late Majesty, I told him, I remembered him in fine hair of his own, which became him better than that of possibly some lewd women, which he then wore.

Before I was relieved, the French drew nearer to our army, and were engaged by some of the troops of the allies; I heard the cannon play, and the small shot rattle about me, which, at first, threw me into a sort of panic, having not been used to such rough music: however, I recovered from my fear, and being ordered by Lord Cholmondeley to repair instantly to my regiment, as I was going, I received a wound from a musket-ball, which grazed on my leg, a little above the ankle, but did not hurt the bone. Lord Cholmondeley was present, and ex-pressed his concern for my wound in very humane terms, ordering me at the same time to be carried off the field.

A short account of this battle may not be disagreeable to my read-ers, since it is possible they will nowhere find one more impartial; that given by the French, being too vain, and the relations we have from the English writers, lessening too much the loss we there sustained.

The Duke of Luxemburg having invested Huy, the 18th of July, 1693, King William, to make a diversion, detached the Prince of Wir-temberg with twenty battalions and forty squadrons, which forced the French lines in Flanders, and put the country under contribution. This detachment, and another the king had sent off to cover Liege, greatly weakened our army. Luxemburg, who had just carried Huy, laid hold on so favourable an opportunity, and drawing together all his forces, as if he had a design upon Liege, on the 28th, about four in the after-noon, presented himself before the allies, who being sensible that they were much the weaker, had posted themselves between the Geete and the brook of Landen.

The fatigue of a long march, and the day being so far spent, made him defer the battle to the next day; but this delay gave King William an opportunity to have secured his troops, by retiring in the night to Zoutleeuw, but His Majesty rather choosing to wait the enemy, fortified the front of his camp, guarded all the passes, placed his cannon to the greatest advantage, and in a word, took all possible precaution to give the French general a warm reception.

At four the next morning the French advanced in good order, within cannon-shot of our intrenchments, that they might have time to raise their batteries; after which, the battle began at the village of Laar, with the left wing of our army, where a terrible slaughter was made. The foot, which were posted behind the intrenchments, suffered the enemy to advance very near to our cannon, and then firing upon them, covered the field with dead bodies, and swept down whole battalions, which lay dead in the same ranks and order as they advanced. The French, notwithstanding, made two vigorous attacks, but did not get an inch of ground upon us, and their obstinacy only augmenting their loss, they gave over on that side about eleven o'clock, but it was to begin again with equal violence with our right wing, which was posted at the village of Neerlanden.

The enemy here met with the same reception, and being repulsed, they made so considerable a movement backwards, that we thought them quite dispirited, and sick of the undertaking; but they, leaving some troops to keep the main body and our left in play, marched with the major part of their forces, and their cannon, to the village Laar, to make one more attack upon our left wing, which was both more vigorous and bloody than the two preceding. The allies defended themselves with equal bravery, till borne down by numbers, they were forced to abandon the village Laar, and the ground between the intrenchment and the brook. The French horse having by this advantage an opportunity to extend themselves, trod under foot all that opposed their passage, and fell upon the rear of the infantry which defended the trenches.

As it was now impossible to drive them out of the post they had won, King William, seeing all efforts vain, ordered the retreat to be sounded. Some few corps retreated in good order, and without confusion, which were mostly Dutch, but the rest took to flight in such disorder and precipitation, that the bridge broke down, and the enemy made bloody havoc of us; whole regiments threw themselves into the Geete, to gain the opposite side, and such numbers were drowned, that their bodies made a bridge for their flying companions, and saved them from the fury of the conquerors. The king, indeed, lost the battle with about sixteen thousand men, the French say twenty thousand, seventy-six cannon, and ninety colours, but he lost nothing in point of reputation. For Lewis XIV. could not help giving him the praise of a great general and brave prince, saying, that, Luxemburg had, indeed, attacked like a Prince of Condé; but, that the Prince of Orange had made his retreat like a Marshal Turenne; and the Prince of Conti, in a letter he wrote to his princess, said, that King William exposing himself with such heroic bravery as he did in this battle, deserved the quiet possession of a crown which he wore with so much glory; and, indeed, the king not only performed the part of a general, but even of a subaltern officer, for he alighted no less than four times to lead on the foot to the attack; and was at the head of the squadron, commanded by Lord Galway, in the hottest part of the battle; he had two led horses killed by him, and a musket-ball went through his sash. It is true, on account of my wound, I could not be an eyewitness of what I have related; but as I was in the army, on the spot, I had it from those who were.

I was two months incapable of service; after which I joined my regiment, which was under cover the remaining part of the summer, and at the approach of winter was ordered into quarters at Gertrudenburg.

While I stayed here, the dikes near the town were ruined by worms, and a village near our quarters was drowned. As the repairing the damaged dikes required the utmost expedition, the English soldiers were commanded to assist the Dutch, and we were obliged to work day and night up to our waists in water, till they were repaired. Lieutenant Gardiner and I staying, the last time we were at the work, somewhat too long, being resolved to see everything secure, narrowly escaped drowning by the tide coming upon us; however, we supported each other, and waded out hand-in-hand, long after the others had gone off.

The following summer was spent in marches and countermarches to watch the motion of the French. During this peaceful campaign, as we were foraging, the French came unexpectedly upon, and took three-score of us prisoners, stripped us, and, by very tiresome marches, conducted us to St. Germain's en lay. The first night, the Dutch and English were promiscuously imprisoned, but the next day King James's queen caused the English to be separated, to have clean straw every night, while the Dutch had none, and allowed us five farthings a day per head, for tobacco, a whole pound of bread, and a pint of wine a day for each man; and, moreover, ordered our clothes to be returned us. The other prisoners had but half a pound of bread a day, drank water, and lay almost naked, in filthy dark prisons, without other support.

The Duke of Berwick frequently came to see that we were well used, and not defrauded of our allowance. He advised us to take on in the French service, as seven of the English did: he spoke to me in particular; I answered, that I had taken an oath already to King William, and if there was no crime in breaking it, as I was satisfied it was one of the blackest dye, I could not in honour break my engagement, nothing in my opinion being more unbecoming an honest man and a soldier, than to break even his word once given, and to wear a double face. He seemed to applaud my principles, and only added, that if I had accepted conditions, I should have been well used; but the choice depended entirely on me.

Captain Cavenaugh, who was my first cousin, and an officer in the French troops, often came to the prison, and I was at first apprehensive of his knowing me; but afterwards, had an inclination to discover myself to him, as I certainly had done had my husband been dead, or had I found him; but my fear of such a discovery being an impediment to the search of my husband, got the better of my inclination.

In about nine days after our imprisonment, Mr. Van-Dedan, a trumpet, and now living in Chelsea, came to exchange us against some French prisoners, and we were set at liberty; after which, as it was a duty incumbent on us, we went to the palace to return Her Majesty grateful thanks for the good offices she had done us, and, indeed, we were greatly indebted to her charity. She had the condescension to see us: she told me, I was a pretty young fellow, and it grieved her much that I had not my liberty sooner.

At our return to the army, we heard the melancholy news of the death of Queen Mary, on which our drums and colours, &c., were put into mourning, and we soon after drew off into winter-quarters. I was in Gorcum, where my grief for my husband being drowned in the hopes of finding him, I indulged in the natural gayety of my temper, and lived very merrily. In my frolics, to kill time, I made my addresses to a *burgher's* daughter, who was young and pretty. As I had formerly had a great many fine things said to myself, I was at no loss in the amorous dialect; I ran over all the tender nonsense (which I look upon the lovers' heavy cannon, as it does the greatest execution with raw girls) employed on such attacks; I squeezed her hand, whenever I could get an opportunity; sighed often, when in her company; looked foolishly, and practised upon her all the ridiculous airs which I had often laughed at, when they were used as snares against myself. When I afterwards reflected on this unjust way of amusement, I heartily repented it; for it had an effect I did not wish; the poor girl grew really fond of me, and uneasy when I was absent; for which she never failed chiding me if it was but for half a day.

When I was with her, she always regaled me in the best manner she could, and nothing was too good or too dear to treat me with, if she could compass it; but notwithstanding a declared passion for me, I found her nicely virtuous; for when I pretended to take an indecent freedom with her, she told me, that she supposed her tenderness for me was become irksome, since I took a method to change it into hatred. It was true, that she did not scruple to own she loved me as her life, because she thought her inclination justifiable, as well as lawful; but then she loved her virtue better than she did her life. If I had dishonourable designs upon her, I was not the man she loved; she was mistaken, and had found the ruffian, instead of the tender husband she hoped in me.

I own this rebuff gained my heart; and taking her in my arms, I told her, that she had heightened the power of her charms by her virtue; for which I should hold her in greater esteem, but could not love her better, as she had already engrossed all my tenderness; and, indeed, I was now fond of the girl, though mine, you know, could not go beyond a platonic love. In the course of this amour, a sergeant of our regiment, but not of the company I belonged to, sat down before the citadel of her heart, and made regular approaches, which cost him a number of sighs, and a great deal of time; but finding I commanded there, and it was impossible to take it by a regular siege, be resolved to give a desperate assault, sword in hand.

One day, therefore, while I was under arms, he came to her, and without any previous indication of his design, a fair opportunity offering, he very bravely, and like a man of honour, employed force to obtain what he could not get by assiduity. The girl defended herself stoutly, and in the scuffle she lost her cap, and her clothes were most of them torn off her back; but notwithstanding her resolute defence, he had carried the fortress by storm, had not some of the neighbours opportunely come in to her assistance, alarmed by her shrieks, and made him retreat in a very shameful manner.

No sooner had she recovered, and dressed herself, than she went in search of, and found me, in my rank, standing to my arms. She told me what had passed, and begged me to revenge the insult offered her. I was so irritated at this account, that I could hardly contain myself: I was seized with a tremor all over my body; often changed colour, and, had I not been prevented by my duty, I should that instant have sought and killed him. However, I stifled my resentment till I was dismissed by the officer, and then went in quest of my rival, whom having found, I surlily asked, how he durst attempt the honour of a woman, who was, for aught he knew, my wife; to whom he was sensible I had long made honourable love. I told him, the action in itself was so base, that it made him unworthy of the king's cloth, which he wore, and ought to be the quarrel of every man in the regiment, as it cast a reflection on the whole corps; but, as I was principally concerned in this insult, so I was sufficient to chastise his impudence, and required immediate satisfaction for the affront. He answered me, that I was a proud, prodigal coxcomb.

'I leave,' said I, 'Billingsgate language to women and cowards; I am not come to a tongue-battle, Mr. Sergeant, but to exact a reparation of honour. If you have as much courage in the face of a man, as you have in assaulting defenceless women, go with me instantly to that windmill (which I pointed to), and I will soon convince you that General T——n had too good an opinion of you, when he took his livery off your back to put on the king's, and gave you a halberd.'

The fellow had been footman to General T——n, and this reproach stinging him to the quick, he only told me, he would soon cool my courage; and we went together to the windmill, where we both drew. I was so irritated at the ill-usage of my sweetheart, and the affront put upon me in her person, that I thought of nothing but putting the villain out of the world. We both drew, and the first thrust I made, gave him a slant wound in his right pap, which had well nigh done his business. He returned this with a long gash on my right arm, (for his sword was both for cutting and thrusting, as all soldiers' swords are; I fought with that I had purchased in Dublin,) but before he could recover his guard, I gave him a thrust in the right thigh, about half a span from the pope's eye; the next pass, he aimed at my breast, but hit my right arm; though it was little more than a small prick of a pin, he being feeble with the loss of blood which flowed plentifully from his wounds.

29

By this time some soldiers on duty having seen our first attack, a file of musketeers, under the command of a sergeant, came up, took us prisoners, disarmed both, and sent him directly to the hospital, and, as my wounds were slight, as I was the aggressor, and beside, a common soldier, conducted me to prison, for the sergeant was thought mortally wounded, and did not recover of a considerable time. I sent my sweetheart an account of what had happened, and where I then was. She acquainted her father with the villainous attempt which the sergeant had made upon her, and let him know it was her quarrel, which I had taken up, was the cause of my confinement. The good *burgher* made a proper representation of the affront offered his family, and found means, in four days' time, to procure me a pardon from King William, an order to release me immediately; to return me my sword, pay my arrears, and give me my discharge from the regiment; all which were punctually performed.

The minute I was enlarged, I went to thank my deliverer for my liberty; she, on her side, as gratefully acknowledged my risking my life in revenging the insult done her. She expressed herself with great tenderness, and told me, that when she heard of my imprisonment, she heartily repented her having acquainted me with the sergeant's villainous attempt; blamed herself for having exposed me to so great a danger, and wished she had buried the action in silence. She proceeded. 'It had been prudent in me, for the sake of both; for you would not have ventured your life, and I should not have given the ill-natured part of the world any ground to censure my conduct; for what interpretation may it not make of your being warm in my cause? This consideration makes me throw off the restraint our sex lies under, and propose to you what I have expected from you, the screening my honour by our marriage.'

'My dear,' said I, 'you offer me the greatest happiness this world can afford me; will you give me leave to ask you of your father?'

'My father!' cried she; 'you cannot imagine a rich *burgher* will give his daughter to a foot-soldier; for though I think you merit everything, yet my father will not view you with my eyes.'

This answer I expected, and, indeed, my being very sure that her father would not consent, was the reason why I proposed speaking to him. I asked her, since she imagined her father would be averse to my happiness, what could be done? 'I will,' said she, 'run the hazard of your fortune, in case my father proves irreconcilable after our marriage.'

30

'My dear life,' said I, 'there are two obstacles to such a proposal, which are, with me, insuperable. How could I bear to see you deserted by your father, deprived of a fortune, and stripped of all the comforts of life, exposed to hardships and insults, to which women who follow a camp are liable? And how can I, with honour, consent to bring your father's grey hairs to the grave in sorrow, by robbing him of a daughter whom he tenderly loves, by way of return for having procured my liberty? No, my charmer, though I am no more than a common sentinel, this breast is capable of as much tenderness, and contains as much honour, as that of a general. No, I can neither be so inhuman to you, nor so unjust to your parent.

'But, as I shall know no satisfaction in life, if deprived of you, it will animate me to such actions, as shall either raise me to a rank that your father need not be ashamed of my alliance, or shall put an end to a life, which must be miserable without you. The sword, my dear, ennobles, and I don't despair of a commission, as I have some reputation in the army, many friends, and am not destitute of money. I think it more becoming the character of a soldier to gain a commission by his bravery, than to purchase one with money: but my desire to call you mine, will make me, at any rate, endeavour to deserve you, and I will, if possible, purchase a pair of colours.'

'I have heard,' said she, 'that love and reason are incompatible; this maxim is either false, or you are not the ardent lover you profess yourself. However, I relish your proposal of buying a commission, and if your money falls short, let me know it.'

'You call,' said I, 'the ardour of my passion in question, because I love you for yourself; I wish to make you, if possible, as happy in our union as I shall be; while most other men have their own satisfaction alone in view, when they address the fair sex. I accept your offer with a grateful sense of the obligation; but hope I need not put you to the proof of your friendship, without some misfortune should deprive me of what I have by me.'

Thus I got off from this *amour* without loss of credit. As I was discharged from my regiment, and loath to break into my capital stock, which would not long maintain me, I entered with Lieutenant Keith, in Lord John Hayes's regiment of dragoons: for my discharge from my regiment was a favour done me, lest the sergeant, by being an officer, and in favour with his quondam master, might do me some private injury: it was not a discharge from the service.

I went to, and stayed in, my lieutenant's quarters, till the season for

31

action came on; when we were all ordered to the siege of Namur.

The army was now more numerous than it had been any preceding campaign; the major part were encamped at Deinse, and seemed to intend an attack upon the French lines, which were in those quarters; this feint, and the Duke of Wirtemberg's assaulting Fort Knoque, drawing most of the French forces on that side, King William, with the greatest expedition, invested Namur, which they had no notion he would sit down before. This motion, however, could not be made with speed enough to prevent Marshal Boufflers from throwing himself into the town with seven regiments, which augmented the garrison to about fourteen thousand effective men. This did not deter the king from prosecuting his design, leaving only thirty thousand men under the command of Prince Vaudemont, to observe the motion of the French, and cover Flanders.

The enemy being well informed of this disposition of the army which was encamped at Woutergen, resolved to attack it in front and flank. The prince making a show of waiting for them, sent his baggage to Ghent, intrenched his camp, placed cannon in all the passes, and taking advantage of the night to prepare for his retreat, made it in the sight of the enemy's army, which advanced to cut him to pieces. The prince had given out such good orders, that all the attacks of the French proved fruitless, and he had the honour of making a glorious retreat, in spite of the enemy, without sustaining any loss. This retreat of Prince Vaudemont is talked of, not only to the present time, but will be admired and looked upon as a masterstroke in ages to come.

He soon after gave a new proof of his martial skill and conduct, in defeating the design which Marshal Villeroy had formed of besieging Nieuport; but the marshal revenged himself on Dixmude and Deinse; the governors of which places wanted courage to defend them, which puts me In mind of a proverb, that it is better to have a lion at the head of an army of sheep, than a sheep at the head of an army of lions.

The king opened the trenches before Namur, in two different places, on the 13th of July, 1695, and, without giving himself any pain about the loss of Dixmude and Deinse, he gave so many assaults to the town, one on the neck of another, and in every assault sent such a number of forces, that they seemed rather small armies than detachments.

The town capitulated on the 4th of August, but the French, to save the citadel, bombarded Brussels; the effect this had, was only making the allies redouble their efforts at Namur. Never was a more terrible fire seen; for no less than sixty large battering-pieces, and as many mortars, played incessantly on the outworks, which rose one above another in form of an amphitheatre. Marshal Villeroy, judging very rightly that the citadel could not hold out long, though defended by a marshal of France, and a numerous garrison, and finding his bombarding of Brussels could not draw off the king, resolved to attack him in his lines, to save the castle, if possible: to this end, ordering several days' provision for his troops, he began his march in a continual rain, and passing by Gemblours, encamped at Saunier, stretching his right towards Conroy, and his left on the side of Granlez. Prince Vaudemont, with the army under his command, had left Brussels, before this motion of the French, to cover the siege; and being joined by some detachments, which had occupied several posts, under the command of the Duke of Wirtemberg and the Earl of Atlilone, he extended his forces behind Mehaigne, as far as from St. Denis to Ipigney.

The French finding him so strongly intrenched that it was impracticable to attack him, turned off to the left, and, going up the Mehaigne, took post on the bank of that river, at Grandrosiers, between the villages of Peruwes and Ramillies; which obliged the allies to advance on the other side as far as Ostin to dispute the passage. As Villeroy was under a necessity to pass the river to succour the besieged, he came very near to us to reconnoitre, and attempted several times to pass, but did not succeed. On this he called a council of war, and gave all the officers liberty to speak their sentiments freely on the means necessary to be taken to succour the citadel. They unanimously declared the thing impossible, and that it would be rash to attempt it.

In the interim, the allies detached thirty squadrons, commanded by Monsieur de la Forêt, who advanced within pistol-shot of the enemy, to reconnoitre. These were discovered by the French scouts, who fell upon them, and, finding they gave way, suffered themselves to be decoyed into an ambush, where the fight renewing with greater fury, the assailants were driven back towards their camp, after they had lost a hundred and fifty horse. After this skirmish, the marshal seeing no likelihood of passing the Mehaigne, or of succouring the citadel, raised his camp, and took post with his army between Chatelet and Charleroy.

Before this retreat of the marshal, most of the fortifications of Namur were demolished, and the breaches made were large enough for a battalion to mount in front; wherefore orders were given for an assault, which was begun on the 30th of August, after the batteries had played with greater fury than ever, from break of day to one and a half afternoon. My Lord Cuts, with three thousand English, was commanded to assault the new castle. Count Rivera, with two thousand Dutch and a thousand Bavarians, was ordered to attack on the side of Fort Koehoorn, while Monsieur la Cave should assault it in front. At the same instant Monsieur Schwerin, at the head of two thousand men, was to assault the covered way before the Devil's House; and, to prevent sallies, a colonel, with five hundred men, was posted between the new castle and Fort Koehoorn.

The signal being given, those troops marched to the assault with incredible intrepidity. Here our brave English were drawn into a fatal mistake by their courage; for three hundred of them mounted the breach of the new castle with such impetuosity, that they could not be supported; by this ardour we failed in the attack of that work. The other assault proved more successful. We carried all the covered way of the Devil's House, and that of Fort Koehoorn. Here we made our lodgements, which being joined, we were masters of three thousand yards of covered way.

Notwithstanding we lost a thousand men in this assault, and had as many wounded, the king was preparing for a second; but Marshal Boufflers, not thinking it expedient to give him the trouble, beat the chamade. Hostages being exchanged, the articles were agreed upon, and the allies took possession, on the evening of the 1st of September, of Fort Koehoorn, some works on that side, and of the breach of the new castle.

On the 5th, the garrison, which still consisted of five thousand one hundred and sixty-eight men, marched out at the breach, with drums beating, matches lighted, colours flying, six pieces of cannon and two mortars, through a lane of thirty battalions of our troops.

The King of France having not only refused to ransom the garrisons of Deinse and Dixmude, but even—sent them towards the frontiers of Spain; King William by way of reprisal, when Marshal Boufflers came out at the head of the light horse, ordered him to be arrested and carried back into the town; where he was told, that if he would give his word that those garrisons should be released, he was at liberty. Upon his refusal, he was conducted to Maestricht, where he was nobly entertained during the time of his confinement, which was but short; for the king, his master, permitting him to promise that those prisoners should be released, he was set at liberty, and conducted by a detachment of two hundred dragoons to Dinant.

After the taking Namur, I went into winter-quarters at the Boss, where a very odd adventure befell me. I went with two of my comrades to a house of civil recreation, where they made a bargain for, and retired with, such ware as they wanted, and I diverted myself with serenading them on the tongs and key. A lady of civil conversation, who was very big, happened to take a liking to me, and used all the common methods of those virtuous damsels to entice me; but finding they had no effect, she swore she would revenge the slight, which she soon after did, by swearing me the father of her child. Whether this was the effect of her revenge, or her judgement, as I made a better figure than any private dragoon in our regiment, and she thought me the best able to provide for her in her month, and to take care of her bastard, is what I won't take upon me to determine; but I was so surprised and enraged at the impudent perjury, that I was almost tempted to disprove her effectually, and give her up to the law; but, on a mature deliberation, I thought it better to defray the charge, and keep the child, which I did; but it died in a month, and delivered me from that expense, though it left me the reputation of being a father, till my sex was discovered.

As nothing remarkable happened to me from this time, to the signing of the peace, it may not be ungrateful to give some memoirs of what passed in the interim in Flanders, where I continued in the same regiment till the army was disbanded.

King William arrived in Holland on the 17th of May, 1696, with design to open the campaign in the Low Countries. The army being thus disposed, a part of the Dutch troops were drawn together near Tirlemont, under the command of Prince Nassau-Sarbruck, field-marshal of the States, who, conjointly with the Elector of Bavaria, was to observe the French forces encamped at Fleuris. The other part of the Dutch army, under the command of Prince Vaudemont, was posted at Destelberg, near Ghent, to oppose Marshal Villeroy, who, with part of the French army, had encamped at Deinse. The king joined the Prince of Vaudemont's army in the beginning of June, and having taken a general review on the 7th, he ordered several forts to be raised on the ways to Marikerque and Nieuport, to cover the canal on that side.

In the meanwhile, the troops of Liege and Brandenburg being arrived at the camp of Tirlemont, this body of the army marched on the side of Brussels, stretching the right as far as Limale, and the left to Otterburg. King William, joined with some troops, after having encamped on the plain of Corbais from the 18th of June to the 7th of July, marched directly towards Noirmont and Gemblours. All these motions were both to observe the French, and to have the conveniences, for a considerable part of the campaign, to subsist the army from Brussels.

All this while Marshal Villeroy remained quiet in his camp, near Deinse, between the Scheld and the Lys; and, having extended his left along this small river, and his right towards Cruyshouten, within two leagues and a half of Oudenard, he secured the forage, and maintained a considerable part of his troops at the expense of the enemy: so that King William finding nothing could be done, he sent back the German troops commanded by the *landgrave* of Hesse, went to Mecklin, and from thence to Loo.

The King of France, whose subjects were miserably harassed, had some time before made propositions of peace to the allies, of whom the duke of Savoy was considerably the least powerful, yet having so great a support, he was the most formidable, because the French provinces bordering on his country, having no strong towns, were exposed to an invasion. This made Lewis of opinion, that he ought, at any price, to clap up a peace with this prince; wherefore, he covertly offered to give him Pignerol; restore all the conquests he had made upon him in the course of the war, and, to strengthen their union, to marry his grandson, the Duke of Burgundy, to Mary Adelaide, the Duke of Savoy's daughter.

These offers were so very advantageous, that they staggered the duke; however, the reproachful shame which must necessarily have been the consequence of his breaking through solemn engagements, by which he had obtained immense sums from the states–general, and other allies, made him, for some time, hold out against the temptation: but France, always productive of expedients, soon furnished him with a plausible pretence. She acted on the defensive only in Catalonia, Germany, and the Low Countries, that she might turn the greater part of her forces upon Savoy.

On the 15th of May, N. S., this same year, Marshal de Catinat entered Piedmont, and pushing forward into the country, came to Rivalta on the 2nd of June. This place is but two leagues' distance from Turin. The duke, upon his approach, cut down the trees, armed all the peasants, and drew the auxiliary troops out of his garrisons, as if he had designed to oppose the enemy. Notwithstanding all these preparations for a vigorous defence, no hostilities were committed on either side.

At length, the proclaiming a suspension of arms for thirty days discovered the mystery of this inactivity, which caused the surprise of every one of the allies. This truce was twice renewed, and at length attended by a treaty of peace, proclaimed in Paris on the 10th of September. At the same time that Lewis XIV. was carrying on his intrigue with Savoy, he made advantageous offers to King William and the states; to which the latter began to listen. In a word, a congress was opened on the 9th of May, 1697, N. S., at Ryswick.

Notwithstanding the conferences for the pacification of Europe were carried on in Holland, there was no suspension of arms; for, on the 16th of May, the French besieged Ath, a town in Hainault. King William being arrived from England, immediately went to the army of the allies; we were no less than a hundred thousand effective men, whom he headed, and marched to St. Quentin Lennich, where a body of eleven thousand Germans were ordered to join us, to save Ath, if possible: but the besiegers were so well intrenched, and covered by two armies under the command of Boufflers and Villars, that we could not force them without visible danger, and exposing Brussels to a second bombardment.

These obstacles obliging King William to withdraw with a part of the army to Gemblours, and the Elector of Bavaria, with the other to Deinse, Ath surrendered on the 1st of June, N. S.

The conferences at Ryswick ended in peace, which was signed by the deputies of the states in conjunction with King William, and by the French plenipotentiaries, on the 20th of September. The King of England ratified this peace on the 20th. It was proclaimed in Paris the 23rd of October, and in London on the 28th, O. S.

The King of England having reviewed the army on the plain of Breda, we were disbanded, and I set out for the Brill, took my passage on board a ship bound for, and arrived safe in Dublin. On inquiry, I found my mother, children, and friends, wanted neither health, nor the necessaries of life. I found means to converse with them; but I was so much altered by my dress, and the fatigues I had undergone, that not one of them knew me, which I was not sorry for. The demand the nurse had upon me, on account of my youngest child, being greater than suited with my circumstances to discharge, I resolved to remain *incog.*

I was not long easy in this indolent way of life, which must soon have drained my purse, wherefore I sought for employment, and found means to support myself, while in Dublin, without breaking into my capital, (which I had hitherto husbanded with great economy,) till the death of the King of Spain, on the 31st of October, 1700; his having in his will declared, through the intrigues of Cardinal Portocarrero, the Duke of Anjou his successor; and his immediately taking possession of those kingdoms, alarmed all the powers of Europe; and the king of France having acknowledged the prince of Wales, King of England, on the death of his father, which happened at St. Germains on the 16th of September, N. S., 1701, grossly affronting King William, seemed to be the harbingers of a new war, as indeed they proved; for it could not be supposed that the emperor would tamely cede his right.

Hostilities were begun in Italy; which Prince Eugene entered in May, 1701, at the head of twenty thousand men; beat the French and Savoyards, who guarded the passage of the Adige, from their posts, and passed the river.

Though none of the powers had declared war, the Hollanders drew together their troops near Rosendaal, under the command of the Earl of Athlone; and the imperialists, commanded by Prince Nassau Sarbruch, *generalissimo* of the emperor, re-enforced by some Dutch troops, besieged Keisersweert.

This news of a war awakened my martial inclination. I was not long considering what party to take; but immediately took shipping for Holland, and finding my quondam Lieutenant Keith, I enlisted with him in my old corps, the regiment of dragoons, under the command of Lord John Hayes.

The first action I was in, was that of Nimeguen, where we were very roughly handled by the French. As this, which deserves rather to be called a battle than an action, would have ruined all the schemes of the allies, had we lost it, I shall give the best account of it I am capable; to do which, I must return to the siege of Keisersweert.

This town, which was very strongly fortified, the Germans invested on the 16th of April, 1702, N. S, The Prussians took post above, and the Dutch below the town, and each of these troops on their respective sides broke ground on the 18th. At the first advice which was given Marshal Boufflers of this siege, he passed the Maes, near Stevensweert, with design to surprise a body of Dutch troops under the command of Count Tilly: but that general being informed of the march of the French, sent all his heavy baggage to Emerick, went to, and encamped at Ebber, within a league of Cleves, where the Earl of Athlone joined him with the rest of the army belonging to the states-general; so that Monsieur Bouffler's design proved abortive. The

Count de Tallard proved more successful in his, which he entered upon a few days after. He took post over against Keisersweert, on the banks of the Rhine; and thus, not only kept open a communication with the town by water, but galled the besiegers so much with his cannon, that they were obliged to quit their works, contract their quarters, and begin new attacks, out of the reach of his cannon. During this siege, the Duke of Burgundy arrived at the French army, to take upon him the command in chief.

Soon after the arrival of this prince, Marshal Boufflers, concluding that the town could not hold out long, resolved to make a diversion to save it. This was to surprise Nimeguen. After having lain some few days quiet in his camp, to give the Count de Tallard, and other forces, time to join him, he decamped from Santin, the 10th of June, and marched immediately to Keverdonk; from whence he marched between Goch and Gennep, designing to continue his route between Mook and Nimeguen, and to fall upon the Earl of Athlone, who was encamped at Clarenbeek, in hopes the confusion that would attend such an unexpected attack, would afford a fair opportunity to surprise Nimeguen.

But the earl having had information of his march, sent away, with all speed, his artillery and heavy baggage, and detached the Duke of Wirtemberg with some troops to take possession of the higher grounds and passes in the neighbourhood of Mook, while he followed with the rest of the army. In coming to the post which he was to defend, the duke discovered the vanguard of the enemy. He diverted them by a retreating fight, till the Earl of Athlone came up to sustain him with the rest of the Dutch army: notwithstanding which, the two enemy armies, in continually skirmishing, made towards Nimeguen; and the French mixing with the Dutch, some of them got, with the latter, into a few of the outworks, and hoped, in the confusion, to push into the town.

Everything seemed to favour their design; for there were no cannon planted on the ramparts; the magazines were locked up, the keys were not to be found, and those who had the care of them, were absent. I remember it was upon a Sunday, and in sermon time. The *burghers* taking the alarm, took to their arms, broke open the magazines, and drew out the cannon, which they mounted and played upon the French. The fire between the two armies, which advanced with equal pace towards the town, was all this while very hot. The French having placed some cannon on a rising ground, made terrible havoc among the Dutch horse, and seized on one of the fortifications called Kykindeport; but a detachment of the Dutch guards, favoured by eight pieces of cannon, which the *burghers* fired upon the French, soon dislodged them.

Marshal Boufflers, who did not expect so stout a defence, finding his project fail, retreated about two o'clock in the afternoon.

In the interim, the siege of Keisersweert, was vigorously and successfully pushed on; and the governor, after having bravely defended the town thirty days, on the 15th of June capitulated. The garrison was conducted to Venlo with all marks of honour.

That I might not break in upon the account of this battle, and the siege of Keisersweert, I made no mention of myself, and of a particular event. About the middle of the siege, a party of horse and dragoons were detached from the army, under the command of Major-General Dompre: I was in the detachment. We fell in with a superior number of the French cavalry, and put them to the run, with a considerable loss on their, and very little on our, side. I had here the good fortune, though in the thickest of the engagement, to escape without hurt, and to be taken notice of by the officers.

Soon after the surrender of Keisersweert, the Prussian troops joined the grand army, and the Earl of Marlborough, about the same time, arrived with those sent by the Queen of England.

After several motions, in which we could never draw the French to a battle, a detachment invested the town and citadel of Venlo, on the 29th of August, in the night. The horse being not employed in, we covered the siege, and were sometimes sent out to forage. The poor peasants fled before us, and leaving their implements of husbandry in the field, my horse trod on a scythe, and was cut in so dangerous a manner, that I despaired of his recovery; though he at length was again fit for service.

Six days after the trenches had been opened before this town, we assaulted the citadel, and with such success, that, after we had carried the covered way, we took it; which obliged the town to capitulate on the 23rd of September.

Stevensweert and Ruremonde were next invested and bombarded, one after another. The former of these bore our fire but two days, the latter three.

The taking all these places, clearing the Maes of the French garrisons as far as Maestricht, their army retired within their lines, and the allies, on the 14th of October, 1702, appeared before Liege. At our approach the French withdrew into the castles; the deputies of the chapter, and of the magistracy, on the same day agreed on a capitulation with the Earl of Marlborough, and the commissioners of the States-general, for the principality of Liege. In the interim, preparations were made to attack the two forts which commanded the town. Three days together we battered the citadel, and the breach being thought sufficient, we assaulted it the 23rd in the afternoon. We soon carried the half-moon, and finding less resistance than we expected, we cleared the palisades, mounted the breach sword in hand, and made a cruel slaughter. The English, in particular, distinguished themselves in this assault; for they mounted at a place called the *Six-cent-pas*, the six hundred steps, for so many there are, and steeper than any pair of stairs I ever saw in my life.

We found in the place above thirty pieces of cannon, and beside twenty thousand florins in silver, a very considerable booty; for the citizens had carried thither their most valuable effects for security. I got but little of the plunder; for the grenadiers, who were in the place, before our dragoons had dismounted, and left their horses to the care of every tenth man, which we do when we fight on foot, were very industrious in their search. I got, however, a large silver chalice, and some other pieces of plate, which I afterwards sold to a Dutch Jew for a third part of their value.

As the citadel was taken by assault, few of the garrison escaped with life, and not one of those who did carried off with them rags enough for a cut finger.

We, after this, attacked the fort of the Carthusians on the other side the Maes. Our batteries began to play the 29th, with great fury; the garrison, terrified by the example made of that citadel, and fearing an assault, in less than three hours asked to capitulate. Articles were that day agreed upon, and the French marched out the next.

The taking of these places proved a great refreshment to the army, for we found a great quantity of good wine, and excellent bread.

Thus ended our first campaign in Flanders; the success of which did not a little raise the hopes of the allies.

I forgot to take notice of the declaration of war; for though hostilities were begun before any was made, yet they were carried on but a little while; for the emperor declared war the 15th of May, 1702, N. S., as did the English queen and the Dutch on the same day.

In Italy, Prince Eugene, in October this year, surprised Cremona, got into the town through an aqueduct, and had kept possession had not the courage of my countrymen, so much despised in England, driven out the Germans; who, however, carried off prisoners Marshal Villeroy, Monsieurs de Mongon, d'Egrigney, and some other persons of distinction. The honour of taking the marshal fell also to an Irishman, captain of horse in the imperial service.

I was ordered into quarters at Venlo, and a night or two afterwards, was one of those commanded by the governor to escort the Earl of Marlborough along the banks of the Maes, the troops which brought him from Ruremond having been dismissed. During our march, by the darkness of the night, we mistook, and going up the country, fell in with a hog-sty, where was a sow with five pigs, one of which I made bold with. I was possessed of it some time, when one Taylor, a corporal, belonging to Brigadier Panton's regiment of horse, attempted to spoil me of my booty; on which some words arising, he drew, and made a stroke at my head, which I warding with my hand, had the sinew of my little finger cut in two; at the same time, with the butt end of my pistol, I struck out one of his eyes. When we returned to our quarters, I got the sinew sewed up.

In the interim, our general was taken prisoner by a party of thirty-five soldiers; but got off by means of a sham pass. The next day we heard of this accident, but not of his having escaped. The garrison, as the earl was entirely beloved by all the forces, was greatly alarmed, and the governor of Venlo, placing himself at our head, marched straight to Guelders, to which place he imagined the earl had been conducted, threatening to come to the utmost extremities if he was not delivered up. In the mean while, he received certain advice of our general being in safety; on which we marched back to our quarters, without attempting any action, and soon after had the joyful news of the queen having rewarded his virtues with the titles of Marquis of Blandford and Duke of Marlborough; on which the rejoicings customary were made, and we were regaled at our bonfires with good liquor.

As we lay quiet all the winter, my husband, whom the hurry of the war had in a manner banished, occurred to my memory, and I made what inquiry I could after him, but in vain; wherefore, I endeavoured, as I concluded him for ever lost, to forget him, as the melancholy the remembrance of him brought upon me, profited him nothing, while it consumed me. To do this, I had recourse to wine and company, which had the effect I wished, and I spent the season pretty cheerfully.

The Duke of Marlborough parted from London in March, 1703, N. S., to put himself at the head of the army, and open the campaign.

He stayed some little time at the Hague, to be present at, and give his advice in the conferences then held; after which he took upon him the command, and invested Bonn on the 24th of April. This town was the residence of the Elector of Cologne, who had received into it a French garrison, for which reason we ravaged the countries of Berg, Cologne, and Cleves, and wasted them with pillaging and contribution.

We opened the trenches before Bonn, and the fort on the other side of the Rhine, the 3rd of May, in the night. Our fire was so brisk, and we pushed on our attacks with so much fury, that the garrison in the fort set fire to their barracks, blew up their magazines, and got into the town sheltered by the smoke. On the 12th, the breach was large enough for a regiment to mount at a time: we carried the covered way, made a lodgement on the palisades, and everything was ready for a general assault; when Monsieur d'Alegre hung out a white ensign. The capitulation was signed that night, and four days after the garrison marched out through the breach, with only six pieces of cannon, and were conducted the shortest way to Luxemburg.

The duke having provided for the security of this place, the greatest part of the troops employed against it marched towards Brabant to join the grand army, which Field-Marshal Auverquerque had drawn together at Maestricht, and which observed the motions of Marshal Boufflers and Villeroy. After this junction, the allies marched towards the lines the French had thrown up from the Scheld to the Maes, near Namur, to cover Brabant.

On the other hand, Baron Spar and Monsieur Coehorn, with a part of the army, put great part of Flanders under contribution. The Grand Army was designed to attack the French lines in Brabant, and in case of succeeding, to, afterwards, besiege Antwerp; and to this end, Baron Obdam had taken post at Ekeren, pretty near that city, with thirteen battalions and twenty-six squadrons. The grand army was marched to encamp before the lines, between Courselle and Beringhen.

The distance between the two armies, and the feebleness of that commanded by the baron, made Boufflers resolve on surrounding him; and accordingly, having placed troops in all the passes through which the Dutch must necessarily retreat, with fifty-three battalions, seventy companies of grenadiers, and fifty-two squadrons drawn out of the neighbouring garrisons, on the 29th of June, in the night, he began his march, which was so secret and expeditious, that the baron, though he had information of the enemy being in motion, had not time to send off his heavy baggage to Bergopsoom; and when he thought of retreating, he found himself enveloped by the enemy, who attacked him so briskly, that his men were driven from the posts they had taken. The baron, being gone some distance from the gross of his troops, to give orders, had the misfortune to have his return cut off, and was obliged to fly to Breda.

The fight, which began at three in the afternoon, grew hotter and hotter; the Dutch taking courage from their despair, being entirely surrounded, and the French being irritated at so obstinate a resistance, when, on account of their great superiority, they flattered themselves with an easy victory. The battle lasted till night, when the Dutch foot beginning to want powder and ball, with their bayonets fixed, attacked and carried the village of Otteren; took one piece of cannon, two kettle-drums, seven colours, with two standards, and passing the night in this village, they retreated in good order to Lillo.

The Battle of Ekeren was very bloody; but the Dutch troops gained more honour in it than their general, who if he did not want courage, could lay no claim to conduct.

It was now resolved, in a grand council of war, since we could not bring the enemy to a battle, which had been often, in vain, offered them, to draw together all the troops dispersed in different posts, and besiege Huy; it being thought too hazardous to attack them in their lines, where they had sheltered themselves.

When our army drew near to Huy, the garrison withdrew into the castle, and we took possession of the town. Before I proceed, I must take notice of one action, which had liked to have slipped my memory. Monsieur de Villeroy, some little time before we opened the trenches before the town, spread it abroad that he would give us battle; upon which our army drew up, but he not liking our countenances, altered his mind, if before he was in earnest, and retired into his lines. Our lieutenant, with thirty of our dragoons, fell in with a party of forty horse of the enemy, but they took to flight at the first fire, and we pursued them to the barriers of their intrenchments; and being there ordered to stand our ground, we maintained it, in the midst of many smart fires, till we had taken a view of the enemy's situation, which was the errand our regiment and some others were sent upon.

The Baron de Trogné opened the trenches before Fort St. Joseph on the 17th of August, N. S., and, the next day, ground was broke before Fort Picard. They surrendered on the 27th, and Count Sinzendorff taking possession of the place for the emperor, we prepared for another siege. Monsieur de Bulau, lieutenant-general of the Hanoverian troops, was, on the 8th of September, detached with twenty-four squadrons to invest Limbourg, and the rest of the troops designed for this siege having joined him, they immediately carried part of the suburbs, and on the 21st took the lower town. As the garrison was pretty much straitened, in what was still in their possession, five battalions were left to blockade and starve them to a surrender; but, tired with this tedious method, on the 26th the besiegers began to batter the place with forty-two pieces of cannon from four batteries, and with twenty mortars. The fire continued very vigorous till about the next day at noon, when the governor seeing great part of the rampart demolished, beat the chamade, and surrendered prisoners of war. However, all the officers were handsomely treated, and nothing taken from them, or even their soldiers, arms excepted.

The Grand Army did nothing more this campaign, than observe the enemy, to favour the Brandenburghers, who were sate down before Gueldre, which they took, after an obstinate defence, having been battered, after a blockade of the whole summer, with fifty-one pieces of cannon, twenty culverins, and twenty mortars, which reduced the town to a heap of rubbish, from the 7th of October to the 17th of December.

The emperor having made cession of his right to the Spanish monarchy, to his elder son the King of the Romans, and he again to the archduke his brother, who was set out to take possession of Spain, the Duke of Marlborough left the army, and set out for the Elector Palatine's court, to meet and compliment the new king, Charles III., in the name of our queen.

The success attending the arms of the French and the Elector of Bavaria in Germany, alarming England and Holland, they resolved to seek them, even in the heart of Germany. To this end, their forces, about the end of April, 1704, were assembled upon the Maes, between Venlo and Maestricht, where we were joined, in the beginning of May, by the Duke of Marlborough and Field-Marshal Auverquerque. After a council of war had been held, the army was divided into two corps, one of which, strong enough to make head against the French in the Low Countries, was left under the command of Monsieur Auverquerque, and the other, commanded by the Duke of Marlborough, passing the Rhine, the Main, and the Nekre, by long and tiresome marches, which greatly harassed our foot, made for the Danube. I cannot help taking notice in this place, though it breaks in upon my narrative, of the Duke of Marlborough's great humanity, who seeing some of our foot drop, through the fatigue of the march, took them into his own coach.

The French, following the example of the allies, drew twenty thousand men out of the Low Countries, who began their march the 18th of May, and passed by Luxemburg to re-enforce the Elector of Bavaria in Germany, under the command of Villeroy. But, before he came to the end of his march, the Duke of Marlborough had joined the Prince of Baden at Lutshausen, which obliged the elector to withdraw to Dilling, a very advantageous post, and strongly fortified, leaving eighteen of his regiments, and eight squadrons, with the Count of Arco, who posted himself on the hill of Schellenberg by Donawert, in intrenchments in a manner inaccessible, that he might cover Bavaria. The resolution was, notwithstanding, taken to attack him, and to open a passage, by forcing his post, to the very heart of the electorate.

We decamped the 2nd of July from Onderingen, and advanced to Ubermargen, within a league of Donawert; but our vanguard did not come in sight of the enemy's intrenchments till the afternoon: however, not to give the Bavarians time to make themselves yet stronger, the duke ordered the Dutch general, Goor, who commanded the right wing, composed of English and Dutch, with some auxiliary troops, to attack, as soon possible: thus we did not stay for the coming up of the imperialists. We began about six o'clock, and were twice repulsed, with very great loss; but this did not abate anything of our courage; our men, rather animated by this resistance, gave a third assault, at the time the Prince of Baden arrived with the German troops of the right wing, who attacked on his side.

The slaughter, which was very great, had lasted above an hour, when the Duke of Wirtemberg had the good fortune, with seven squadrons, to enter the enemy's trenches, by the covered way of Donawert, and fell upon their rear. The Bavarians were now soon routed, and a cruel slaughter made of them, and the bridge over the Danube breaking down, a great number were drowned, or taken prisoners. In the second attack, I received a ball in my hip, which is so lodged between the bones that it can never be extracted; to this day the wound is open, and has almost deprived me of the use of my leg and thigh.

Captain Young, who, poor gentleman, was soon after killed, desired me to get off; but, upon my refusal, he ordered two of my comrades to take me up, and they set me at the foot of a tree, where I endeavoured to animate my brother soldiers, till I had the pleasure of seeing them get into the trenches and beat down their enemies; though it was a dear-bought victory, as they disputed every inch of ground, and showed an uncommon bravery. We lost, of my acquaintance, Captain Young, Captain Douglass, and Lieutenant Maltary, besides a number of private men.

I was carried to the hospital near Schellenberg, and put under the care of three surgeons, Mr. Wilson, Mr. Laurence, and Mr. Sea, and narrowly escaped being discovered. Here, while I was under cure, I received my share of what plunder was made, which the duke's justice ordered to be impartially distributed among his brave fellow-soldiers. Beside the arms the fugitives threw away, the allies took sixteen pieces of cannon, thirteen standards and colours, all the tents, the baggage and plate of the Count of Arco. This general, when he found his intrenchments entered by the allies, withdrew to Donawert; but the inhabitants not opening the gates soon enough, he was forced to throw himself into the Danube, and had the good fortune to get safe to Augsburg. When the gates of Donawert were set open, those who kept the intrenchments on the side of the town, crowded into it, and at first made a show of defending it; but that evening, having received orders from the elector to burn the town and provisions, to blow up the ammunition, break down the bridges, and retreat to Augsburg, they clapped straw into the houses, to which they began to set fire; but had not time to perfect their design, for fear of their retreat being cut off, the allies being got into the suburbs, and laying bridges over the river, which compelled them to withdraw at four o'clock in the morning, and gave the *burghers* an opportunity to save the town.

The allies entered it, and therein found three pieces of cannon, twelve pontons of copper, twenty thousand weight of powder, three thousand sacks of flour, quantities of oats, and other provisions. These were the fruits of our victory, which, however, we purchased by the loss of three thousand brave fellows killed and wounded, and, among several other general officers of distinction, General Goor received a musket-ball in his eye, and instantly expired in the arms of Monsieur Mortaigne, who ran to his assistance. The Duke of Luneburg Bevern was mortally wounded, and died before the fight was over.

The allies having garrisoned Donawert, made themselves masters of Rain, by composition, and carried the little town of Aicha sword in hand, where they put five hundred of the garrison to death, and took the rest prisoners. They had now nothing to prevent their piercing to the centre of Bavaria, where they were so greatly alarmed, that the inhabitants of Lechausen, Strottlingen, and Friedbergen, hearing of the defeat at Schellenberg, quitted their houses, and even the Electress of Bavaria did not think herself in safety at Munich, though she had eight thousand men of regular troops; but desired the Archbishop of Saltzburg to give her shelter. Her fear was not groundless; for, after the taking Rain and Aicha, the allies sent parties on every hand to ravage the country, who pillaged above fifty villages, burnt the houses of peasants and gentlemen, and forced the inhabitants, with what few cattle had escaped the insatiable enemy, to seek refuge in the woods.

The elector, who, after the defeat of his troops near Donawert, expected to see his country laid waste, held a council of war in the open field, composed of his generals and most experienced officers; wherein it was resolved immediately to abandon the camp of Lauingen, though very advantageous, and extremely well fortified, and to reinforce the army as much as possible.

In consequence of this resolution, they drew out the Bavarian garrisons of Hochstat, Dilllngen, Lauingen, Neuburg, and of several little towns; after which, their army encamped under the walls of Augsburg, whither they had before sent immense sums under a strong escort, raised by the plunder and contributions of the preceding year. The elector lodged in the convent of St. Uliu, and compelling the *burghers* to work day and night on the intrenchments of his camp, he surrounded it with a ditch fifty feet wide, and proportionably deep, that he might, in greater security, wait the succours Marshal Tallard was leading to him.

The event proved, that the elector was in the right to depend on succour from France; for the two marshals, Villeroy and Tallard, ordered their march so as to, arrive at Augsburg in the beginning of August. The Prince Eugene, of Savoy, who had hitherto watched them, now joined the grand army, part of which formed the siege of Ingolstadt, under the command of the Prince of Baden. The enemy were, by this siege, drawn out of their intrenchments, and having posted themselves at Hochstat, the allies resolved to decamp from Erlinkhoven, and go thither to attack them, though their right was protected by the Danube, and their left by the wood of Lutzingen, and their fronts by two riviulets and a morass, which entirely sheltered them.

At six o'clock in the morning, on the 13th of August 1704, we came in sight of the enemy, and, about eleven, were drawn up in order of battle; we then threw five bridges, made of fascines and tin pontons, over the rivulet before the faces of the enemy, posted behind it, and at two, the signal was given to attack.

Everyone has read an account of this battle, which was as memorable as that of Crecy, or Agencourt; wherefore it is needless for me to trouble my readers with a detail of it. I shall only take notice of one thing, in honour to that great and glorious English captain, the Duke of Marlborough, which is, that after part of the horse of the left wing of our army had passed with a good deal of difficulty, the rivulet, the rest endeavouring also to pass it, were twice repulsed, which the duke seeing, led them on himself for the third time, and making the enemy give ground, their main battle was defeated, and their right, which opposed the duke, and was of French troops, was driven to the banks of the Danube, and separated from the rest of the army; while the Bavarians twice repulsed our right wing, where Prince Eugene commanded, and had driven him a hundred and fifty feet beyond his first post, which made the duke, who had now his hands at liberty, send a detachment to attack the enemy in the rear, and assist the prince; but before these orders could be put in execution, he had made a fourth attack upon, and put to flight, the Bavarians in the right wing.

After the loss of this battle, the Elector of Bavaria drew his garrison out of Augsburg, and the magistrates immediately sent advice of it to the prince and duke, requiring their protection, which was readily granted.

After the victory of Hochstat, the allies did not think proper to push on the siege of Ingolstadt; wherefore, leaving some forces to keep it invested, the rest marched to reinforce the Grand Army, commanded by Prince Eugene. The English and Dutch, under the command of the Duke of Marlborough, on the 22nd of August, N. S., appeared before Ulm, where the enemies, in their flight, had left a strong garrison under the command of General Bettendorf, both to favour their retreat, and to cut out some work for the allies in those parts. The day of our arrival before this town, the duke ordered the governor to be summoned; who answering, that he would defend the town to the last extremity, a council of war was held, and, according to the resolutions therein taken, the army divided; Prince Eugene and the duke marched with the major part, by different routes, towards the Rhine, and the rest, which were imperial troops, continued in Suabia, under the command of General Thungen, to take in Ulm, and other towns in the possession of the enemy, and to entirely subdue the whole country; which he did.

After the reduction of Ulm, which capitulated as soon as the batteries of the besieged were ready, notwithstanding the resolute answer sent to the duke's summons, the Baron de Thungen joined the grand army under the Duke of Marlborough, which covered the siege of Landau, invested the 13th of September. The King of the Romans, desirous to be at the siege, set out eleven days before from Vienna, of which, advice being come, Prince Eugene and the duke set out to receive him between Philipsburg and Landau, and conducted him through the army, under arms, to his quarters at Ilbesheim.

This town, and all others in which the elector had garrisons, were evacuated by treaty; he himself entirely stripped of his country; his electrice and children made prisoners; his subjects disarmed, and obliged to take an oath of allegiance to the emperor; five thousand men garrisoned in his metropolis, and the estates of such of his subjects as had followed his fortunes, were confiscated. In a word, Bavaria was: treated as a conquered country, and the Count Leuwenstein-Worthem was made governor of it.

I have already said, we miserably plundered the poor inhabitants of this electorate; I had left the hospital time enough to contribute to their misery, and to have a share in the plunder. We spared nothing, killing, burning, or otherwise destroying whatever we could carry off. The bells of the churches we broke to pieces, that we might bring them away with us. I filled two bed-ticks, after having thrown out the feathers, with bell-metal, men's and women's clothes, some velvets, and about a hundred Dutch caps, which I had plundered from a shop; all which I sold by the lump to a Jew, who followed the army to purchase our pillage, for four *pistoles*; beside the above things, as I was not idle, I got several pieces of plate, as spoons, mugs, cups, &c., all which the same conscionable merchant had at his own price.

I might have mentioned this more properly before, but I did not think what regarded me in particular, of consequence enough to break the thread of my narration: and the same reason prevails on me to go back to the siege of Landau, under the command of the king of the Romans, which, after a vigorous defence, surrendered on the 22nd of November. It was invested, as I have already said, the 13th of September.

I now come to my own history. After the Battle of Hochstat, in which I received no hurt, though often in the hottest of the fire, I was one of those detached to guard the prisoners; and surely, of all I ever saw, none were more miserable; some having no shirts, some without shoes or stockings, and others naked as from the womb. In this wretched condition we marched them to the plain of Breda, where we halted to refresh; each man, prisoners and all, being allowed a pint of beer and a pennyworth of bread and cheese.

During our halt here, I was amused with two very different scenes by the women, some of which bewailed the loss of their husbands, or lovers, who fell in the two memorable Battles of Schellenberg and Hochstat; and others congratulating and caressing their spouses and sweethearts who had escaped the danger. Among the latter, I observed a woman, with a visible joy in her face, make up to a man, whom, by his side face, I fancied I had known; I drew near to the palisades where my horse was tied, and looking through at the instant he turned to embrace her, had a full view of, and perfectly knew him, to my un-speakable grief, to be my perfidious husband, on whose account I had experienced so much fatigue, such misery, and had so often hazarded my life.

The seeing him caress the Dutch woman, for such she appeared to be, and really was, raised in me so great an indignation, that I was resolved to banish every tender thought which might plead in his favour, and wipe the idea of him out of my memory. Thus resolved, I turned my back upon them, and had no sooner done it, but I began to think his infidelity rather a misfortune to me than a fault in him, as he had never received any news, or answer to his letters, of which he mentioned twelve in the only one I received. I was so divided between rage and love, resentment and compassion, that the agitation of my mind had such a visible effect on my body, and was so plainly discernible in my countenance, that my comrade asked me what it was that troubled me, that I changed colour, and trembled as I did, all over me. I had a pot of beer in my hand, and had not power to utter more than. 'Take the beer, I can hold it no longer.'

After some little time, I recovered my spirits, and answered, that I saw my brother, Richard Welsh (I had often declared I had such a brother in the army, of whom I could hear no news) standing in the foremost rank of Lord Orkney's regiment of foot, and that I had not seen him of twelve years before; this sudden and unexpected sight of a lost brother, occasioned the disorder in me he had remarked. I then pointed him out, and begged my comrade to step and ask him if his name was not Richard Welsh, and when he had heard from his wife and children. He readily complied with my request, and, as I could not take my eye off him, I saw my comrade accost him, and immediately return with this answer, that as he was the first man upon command,

I might speak to him at the main guard: hardly had he delivered these few words, when the drums and trumpets gave us notice to march for Breda, from whence we were distant about a league, though it appeared to me ten times as long, so uneasy was I, and anxious to speak to him, and hear what he could say in his vindication.

On our arrival at Breda, we were obliged to house our prisoners, whose number was so great, that it compelled us to the making prisons of workhouses, and even of those of private people. After my duty was performed, I went in search of my husband to the main guard, where I learned that he was at a public house behind it. I immediately followed him thither, and passing through the outward room to the kitchen, saw him there, drinking with the Dutch woman. I took no notice of him, but going up to the landlady, desired to be shown a private room; she accordingly went before me into one backwards, and bringing me a pint of beer which I called for, left me to my own melancholy thoughts. I sat me down, laid my elbow on the table, and leaning my head on my hand, I began to reflect on my former happy situation after the death of my aunt, and of the misfortunes which had attended my love for a man who no longer thought of me, though obliged by the strongest ties of gratitude.

'But,' said I, 'Have I done more than my duty? Is he not my husband? Nay, did he not, till an unforeseen misfortune tore him from me, treat me with the greatest tenderness? Had I once reason to complain of his want of love or gratitude? But why is he thus changed? Here his fondness which I had observed for the Dutch woman, gave vent to my tears, which flowing in abundance, was some relief to me.'

I could not stop this flood; it continued a good quarter of an hour; at length it ceased, and, drinking a little of the *hougarde*, which is a white beer, in colour like whey, I washed my eyes and face with the rest, to conceal my having wept. I did all I could to compose myself, and, calling my landlady, I desired she would bring another pint, and acquaint the young man of Orkney's regiment, drinking in her kitchen, that I desired to speak to him. She delivered my message, and he came in with her. I sat with my back to the light, that he might not see my face plain enough to discover me before I had sounded what interest I retained in his heart. I saluted him by his name, which he civilly returned, and added, that I had the advantage, for he found I knew him, though I appeared a stranger.

'Yes, sir,' replied I, 'you are not unknown to me. Pray when did you hear from your wife and children?'

'Sir,' said he, 'I have heard no news of them these twelve years, though I have written no less than a dozen letters to her, which I am apt to believe have miscarried.'

I answered, that I believe he did not think that a misfortune to lay to heart, since a number of pretty girls here, who were all tender-hearted to the gentlemen of the sword, would easily compensate the absence of, and prevent any concern for a wife; 'you, doubtless, find it so. Sir,' replied he, 'you take me for a villain, and you lie; I do not find it so.'—Not a man in the army would have given me the lie with impunity; but I must own, receiving it from him on such an account, was a greater pleasure to me than if I had been complimented at the head of all our troops by the Duke of Marlborough. A sudden tremor seized me, which he, who had his hand on his sword, taking notice of, and viewing me more intently, discovered that I was his wife.

'Oh heavens!' cried he. 'Is this possible? Is it not delusion? Do I really see my dear Christian? May I believe my eyes?' He ran to me, clasped me in his arms, kissed me in raptures, and bedewed my cheeks with tears of joy.

As soon as I could disengage myself, I replied. 'Yes, Richard, 'tis I, who have been so many years in search of an ungrateful, perjured husband; for, whatever your sex may think of a marriage vow, or properly, though you never think of it at all, the breach of it leaves the foul stain of perjury. What a comfortable reward have I met with for abandoning peace and plenty, could I have known peace without you! for leaving my poor babes, my aged mother, my friends, my relations, and country, to expose myself to the hardships, fatigues, and dangers of a soldier's life, in search of a husband whom I have, at length, found in the arms of another woman! How have I deserved this treatment? What fault of mine, if not my over fondness, could make you cruelly desert me and your children, and rather desperately take up with a life of incessant toil and penury, than continue longer with a wife whom you drove to the utmost despair, by the reasonable belief of your being murdered? as it was impossible for me to think you could make me so barbarous and ungrateful a return for my tenderness.'

'My dear Christian,' said he. 'Do not imbitter the joy I feel in thus meeting with you, by such cruel and undeserved reproaches. Had you received any of my letters, you must have learned my misfortune, not my fault, caused our unhappy separation; for, in every one of them, I gave you a true account.'

'I wish,' said I, interrupting him, 'I had not received that which you said was your twelfth; for my tenderness would not let me believe you capable of a falsity, as I now am convinced you are; it was the fatal receipt of that letter which ruined my peace, by going in search of it. Yes, that letter made me resolve to undergo all dangers, rather than not find you out; had it not come to hand, I might have been still undeceived in the belief of your death; time would have mitigated my grief, and forgetting you, as I am a witness you did me, I might have continued at this time in easy and happy circumstances, have enjoyed the comfort of my friends and relations, and have done my duty to my children, in taking care of their education and settlement, instead of being harassed with fatigues of war, and my poor infants exposed to the hazard of being brought up vagabonds. I have at length found you, but so altered from the just and endearing husband you once were, that I had rather have had assurance of your death, than see you thus survive your affections, which I once was fool enough to believe nothing could take from me.'

'Believe me,' said he, 'my dear Christian, they are still as warm towards you as ever; pardon my faults, which I acknowledge, and make a just distinction between the tender, friendly love for a wife, and the slight, trifling complaisance for such creatures, as may prove our amusement, but can never gain our esteem; and where that is wanting, you are satisfied, however it may be counterfeited, there can be no warm affection.'

'How know I that woman is not your wife?'

He answered, 'No; I own I have my follies, but that does not make me unjust.'

Here the woman, surprised at his stay, came to the door, and, at my bidding, came in, and said, 'My dear, why do you leave me thus alone?' This expression of her fondness threw him into a passion, and he swore that if ever she again used that expression, or followed him more, he would be her death.

'Passion,' said I, 'proceeds very often from, and is a proof of guilt. It is not manly to treat a woman ill, especially if you have, as much I fear, seduced her with a promise of marriage, a practice too customary with our cloth: in such case I shall hold her innocent, if, when she knows you have a wife and children, she breaks off a conversation which will be then criminal in her to continue. Young woman,' said I, 'turning to her, Is this man your husband?'

She answered in the affirmative, which again put him into a passion, and he denied his ever being married to her, with bitter impre-

54

cations. I repeated my question to the woman, who said, indeed the ceremony had not been performed, but that they had been contracted several months, and cohabited, when he was not in the field, as man and wife.

'I am sorry for your misfortune; for this man is married, and has been so many years, to my sister, by whom he has had three children; so that you can have nothing to expect from him but scandal. If you value your reputation or safety, or have any regard for him, avoid him for the future; for I have so great a love for my sister, that if he continued to injure her, I would revenge it as an insult on myself, and expose my life, rather than suffer her to be wronged with impunity. What is passed can no otherwise be redressed than by your being no more guilty; on that condition I forgive you, and will endeavour to forget it.'

The poor woman burst into a flood of tears, and said, no man should have robbed her of her innocence; but she was betrayed by his reiterated promises, backed with solemn oaths, to make her his lawful wife. This he denied as passionately, which made the woman fly into such a rage, and vilify him in such opprobrious terms, that I feared he would do her a mischief, and gave me trouble enough to appease both parties. At length, my temper and reasons brought them to a calm, but it did not stop the woman's tears, who left us weeping, and with a resolution, at least a seeming one, never to come near him more.

When she was gone, I represented to him, in the blackest colours, the villainy of seducing young women by promises of marriage; and told him, that he must account for the breach of such oaths in another life, if he escaped unpunished in this. I told him after this, that notwithstanding the hardships I had gone through, and the wounds I had received, I had such a liking to the service, that I was resolved to continue in it, and, to that end, would pass as his brother, and furnish him with what shirts, or other necessaries, he wanted, while he concealed my sex; but, if ever he discovered me, I would forget he was my husband, and he should find me a dangerous enemy.

'What, then,' said he, 'will you be cruel enough to rob me of my wife? Will you not give me the satisfaction of letting the world know how much you deserve, and how gratefully I can acknowledge the obligation your uncommon love has lain me under? For Heaven's sake reverse so intolerable a sentence! What I have you run so many hazards, borne the fatigue of so many years, only to have the satisfaction of tormenting me? Do you call this love? Banish me your bed.'

I interrupted him with saying, he had forfeited his right to it, by having taken another to his; that my resolution was fixed, and all he could urge would not shake it; therefore desired he would put an end to a vain solicitation, which, if he continued, or ever once renewed, till accident, or peace, discovered me to be a woman, I would never more see him, or be anyway assistant to him.

'Well,' said he, 'I hope time will mollify you; I must obey.'

We sat together some little time after this; then I paid the reckoning, and gave my husband a piece of gold, telling him, he would find me a kind and generous brother, but that he must not think of enjoying his wife, while I could remain concealed, and the war lasted. He embraced me passionately, and telling me he did not think my heart as hard as he found it, we withdrew to our respective posts. We saw and conversed with each other every day, and he would often begin his solicitations, but I immediately put a stop to them. He kept my secret, and, had I not been discovered by an accident, which I shall take notice of in its proper place, I should have continued a dragoon to the end of the war, when I intended, if God spared my life so long, to lay aside my disguise, return to Dublin, and resume my former business.

Having secured our prisoners, we returned to the army, which, under the command of his grace the duke of Marlborough, covered the siege of Landau before mentioned. After the surrender of this town to the King of the Romans, we were ordered to winter-quarters in Holland, leaving the foot, among which was my husband, behind us. His grace having made a tour into Germany, returned to England with his share of the prisoners, standards, and colours, taken at Hochstat,

I obtained leave to visit the Hague, certainly the most beautiful village in the whole world: from thence I made a tour to Rotterdam, and, in the *dragschoot*, happening to sit by a pretty Dutch girl, I told her she was very handsome. She returned, that I was very complaisant, but she did not know anyone to whom she would more willingly appear agreeable; for I was a pretty young fellow.

'I find,' said I, 'your banter will soon silence me; I said that you were handsome, because you are really so, and you are turning me into ridicule for speaking my sentiments; indeed, what I said was needless, because you cannot but be conscious of your own perfections; but out of the fullness of the heart the mouth speaks.'

'The very reason,' replied she, 'that, before I was aware, I spoke my thoughts, which are altogether as sincere as your compliment.'

'Were they so, I should be the happiest man in the whole army of the allies.'

'And, could I make you that happy man, it would, perhaps, make me the most miserable woman.'

'Then you are of opinion that a soldier cannot make a good husband.'

'That is not my reason; it is, I should be in continual apprehension for your life, and never know a minute's peace in your absence.'

'Such a confession might make any man vain, though from a person of much less merit; but I have too great an opinion of your good sense to flatter myself that your heart corresponds with your tongue: no, you thought my declaration impertinent, and you have a mind to revenge yourself, by first raising my vanity, and then laughing at my credulity.'

The *schoot* was, by this time, arrived at Delft; we all went across that town, which is the worst paved in Holland, to take another *schoot* at Amsterdam. I gallanted my pretty *frow* through the street, said all the fine things to her I could think of, and was so importunate to know her place of abode, and to have leave to wait on her, that she let me, at length, know it was without the gate, near the Scotch dike; and added, that if I was sincere, and my intentions honourable, she would give me leave to see her home, when we should come to Rotterdam, and should not be displeased with my future visits. In a word, at our arrival, she gave me her hand to help her out of the *schoot*, and conducted me to her lodgings, where she called for a bottle of wine to refresh me. I drank a glass or two before any but a servant appeared; but, not long after, a sister came in, who embraced her, and asked who I was.

She told her that I was a gentleman belonging to the English forces, (for I had told her, in our passage; she could not otherwise have known, as I was dressed genteelly in a plain suit,) and that she was indebted to me for many civilities. The sister made me a compliment, and said, her mother would thank me, were she not indisposed. On this, my fair one begged me to excuse her waiting on her mother, and, with a surprise, said. The maid told me she was well. I told her I would take a more convenient time to pay her my respects; and, withdrawing, went into the town and got a lodging on the Scotch dike, in a house where a Scotch sergeant, of my acquaintance, going to Scotland to recruit, then lodged. His name was John Beggs; and, since that, he himself kept the same house, and had got money enough, if his good nature, and the credit he gave to any of the three nations, especially if they played at backgammon, had not kept him under to the day of his death.

We were glad to see each other, sapped together, and, over a bottle, I told honest John what a fortunate adventure I had met with in my passage. 'I assure you,' said he, 'you have reason to call it fortunate, for they are mighty virtuous young ladies; there are three sisters and the mother, who live together, and are noted for their extensive charity. I have the honour to be well with, and visit the family: if you consent to it, we will wait on them tomorrow.'

I was glad to hear this character of the family, as I thought I might pass the few days I intended to stay at Rotterdam, in an agreeable, amusing way.

The next morning honest John showed me the town; we saw the town-house and anatomy chamber, the shambles, and the statue of Erasmus, with the house where that great man was born, and then, being tired of rambling, went to our quarters to dinner; after which, we set out to visit my new female acquaintance. We were carried into the same parlour I had been in the evening before. John bid the maid bring a bottle of wine, and tell the lady of the house he was there. I reprimanded him for his freedom, and told him I thought he took as much liberty as if he was in a public house.

'Oh,' said he, 'they allow me to take what liberty I please: they are the best-natured family in Holland.' At that instant my fellow-traveller came in, whom my friend John taking hold of, pulled upon his knee, and she suffered him to take such liberties as convinced me that there was not a family of more extensive charity; for they made no distinctions of rank, nation, or religion. She asked John if I was his acquaintance.

He told her I was; 'Then,' said she, 'as the gentleman made me a great many fine speeches in the *schoot*, and I really like him, do you take my sister, and oblige your friend and me, by my convincing him that I thought him a pretty fellow, as well as said so.'

I was greatly shocked at my disappointment, and had much ado to prevent my treating her in a very rough manner, when she threw her arms round my neck and would have kissed me. I pushed her rudely off, saying, I had mistaken a fiend for an angel. I would have gone directly out of the house, but she clapped herself before the door, and told me, I must first pay the bottle of wine I had the evening before. Upon being told it was a *guder*, I threw down the money, and flew out of the house in a rage; my friend paid the other bottle, and followed me, laughing as if he would never have given over. When he could get the better of his fit, he asked me if I did not think myself fortunate in so virtuous an acquaintance.

Having visited Amsterdam, I returned to my quarters, where I stayed till the opening the campaign of 1705. We marched out of our winter-quarters, and encamped between Maestricht and Liege. The Duke of Marlborough arrived at the Hague on the 14th of April, where he stayed but a few days before he set out to place himself at the head of the army. The foregoing campaign it was agreed to provide good magazines in Germany, which his grace relying upon, took the better part of the army, after he had reviewed us, and directed his march towards the Moselle, to join the Germans betimes, not at all doubting but the French would draw off from the Low Countries a considerable number of their forces, and send them the same way to oppose the allies: but they were too well informed of the neglect of what had been agreed upon; were satisfied the duke would lose a great deal of time in waiting for the Germans, and were therefore determined to take advantage of their delay, and undertake some important expedition on the Maes.

The Dutch army, not being strong enough to keep the field, was intrenched under the cannon of Maestricht. The French, quitting their lines on the 27th of May, encamped at Vegnacourt, and at Val-Nôtre-Dame, and having sent a detachment over the Maes, they, the next day, invested Huy. The town, which was defenceless, immediately surrendered, upon condition that the *burghers* should keep their privileges, that the garrison should have liberty to retire into the castle, and that the French should not fire from the town on the castle nor the others from the castle upon the town. On the 30th, at night, the trenches were opened before Fort Picard, which was carried on the third assault, with all its outworks. They, immediately after the reduction of this fort, with all possible expedition, raised new batteries against the others, and made such a terrible fire with thirty pieces of cannon and twenty mortars, that Cronstrom, who was governor, was obliged to surrender prisoner of war on the 10th of June.

The French taking Huy, and laying siege to the citadel of Liege, together with the want of magazines on the Moselle, (by which neglect the duke's army began to suffer,) and the distance the Germans were off rendering it impossible to join him time enough to undertake any-thing considerable on that side, obliged the duke to quit the Moselle. His grace was no sooner arrived in the neighbourhood of Maestricht, but the French abandoned the city of Liege, raised the siege of the citadel, and withdrew, as usual, into their lines. The army being now united, took the field, and, in few days, retook Huy; and, by the advice of his grace the Duke of Marlborough, resolved to attack the enemy's lines, by the shelter of which they had avoided a battle. To this end we decamped on the 17th of July, and marched straight to their lines, to attack them at one and the same time at Heilisheim, near the village and castle of Wang, and at the villages of Nederhespen and Oostmalen. The vanguard being, at break of day, arrived at the place of rendezvous, Count Noyelles immediately assaulted the castle of Wang, which, after a small defence, he carried, and entering the lines with the runaways, seized on the barriers, and drew up in order of battle.

Three battalions, with the like rapidity, possessed themselves of the village and bridge of Heilisheim, within a quarter of a league of Wang, and took post within the lines. Lieutenant-General Schultz, with as great facility, made himself master of the villages of Overhespen and Nederhespen; by which, our horse and dragoons having openings to enter the lines, his grace led us on, and formed us to make head against the enemy; their corps nearest to the places of attack were in motion at the first alarm, and about fifty squadrons and twenty battalions advanced to dispute the hollow way.

Our horse, sustained by some of the foot, made our way; and the duke, at our head, charged the French horse so briskly, that he broke, entirely routed them, and made himself master of eight pieces of cannon. The rest of the French, who were advancing to support the foremost corps, seeing their horse take to flight, thought it no shame to follow their example. The glorious success of this attack of the French lines, the honour of which, as it was just, every one attributed to the Duke of Marlborough's advice, conduct, and intrepidity, was followed by the taking of Tirlemont, where a French battalion was made prisoners. The French army, which was obliged to retreat, some towards Namur, and others towards Louvain, found means to unite, and intrench themselves behind the Dyle.

The duke would have attacked them here, but being opposed by the Dutch, we had a three days' march for nothing, which the duke resented so much, that the States, to give his grace satisfaction, removed General Schlangenburg, who made the opposition. After we had continued some time in view of the enemy, near the abbeys of Ulierbeek and Park, on the 29th of August the duke marched to Leuwe, which was invested the same day by fifteen battalions, and the same number of squadrons, notwithstanding its situation is in the middle of a morass.

Lieutenant-General Dedem, who commanded this body of troops, having, on the 2nd of September, possessed himself of an advanced redoubt, which was raised on the avenue to the town, between nine and ten that night opened the trenches on the side of the gate of St. Tron, pushed on his works within two hundred yards of the covered way, and the batteries being soon ready to play, the Baron du Mont, who commanded in the place, offered to march out, if all military honours were allowed him. This being rejected, he and his garrison were compelled to yield themselves prisoners of war on the 5th of the same mouth.

Our army having levelled the French lines, broken the sluices, and demolished the outworks of Tirlemont, to prevent the enemy from keeping garrison in it in the winter, we marched to Herenthals, and his grace made a tour to the Hague. On his return to the army, we besieged Sanduliet. The trenches were opened on the 26th of October, and the garrison, in three days, forced to surrender prisoners of war. The taking of this town putting an end to the operations of this campaign, his grace the Duke of Marlborough went to Vienna, and was received with the highest marks of distinction. The emperor confirmed him prince of the empire, erected the district of Mildelheim into a principality for him, and gave advice of it to the *diet* of Ratisbon, enjoining them to receive a deputy of this principality, and to give him place in their sessions. The news of this being brought us, before we left Tirlemont, we were regaled with liquor, and made great rejoicings.

Nothing remarkable, or worth a reader's notice, happened to me in particular this winter. Our recruits, and horses to remount those who had lost them, arrived in Holland the 3rd of April, 1706, and the Duke of Marlborough, with a number of volunteers, landed there on the 25th. The enemy, in the interim, lost no time: they had wrought hard all winter upon their intrenchments behind the Dyle and on the fortifying Louvain, where they had brought together such prodigious quantities of flower, hay, oats, and all sorts of ammunition, that the fifty colleges were quite filled, beside the shambles, convents, &c.

The Duke of Lorrain, fearing his country would be made the seat of war, from his grace's march in 1705 to the Moselle, when he drew near his frontiers, sent the Count Martigny to his grace, with a very complaisant letter; in which he entreated him to use that moderation towards a defenceless country, which had, on many other occasions, heightened his great character. He also acquired of, and obtained from, the King of the Romans, the emperor's protection; and, by a memorial, desired the states-general to observe the same neutrality with regard to him, who was no way interested in the Spanish succession.

His envoy received the following answer to his memorial; That the States having been informed that the French had not only possessed themselves of very advantageous posts in Lorrain, but were actually at work to fortify Nancy, they could not look upon such a procedure as other than an infraction of the neutrality which they had desired the duke to observe, by compelling the French to evacuate those places which they had seized. France, however, was very far from such a disposition; for the king apprehending an invasion, by the way of Lorrain, in the very beginning of this year seized upon all the duke's states, placed garrisons in all his fortified towns, and obliged him to furnish three millions of *livres* yearly, towards the expense of the war.

I thought this little digression necessary, that my readers might be acquainted with the then situation of affairs.

Everything being ready on either side to open the campaign, the army of the allies, on the 22nd of May, encamped between Corris and Tourine, near the stone-mill of Kruisworm: the French also left their intrenchments on the Dyle, with design to surprise us while they were superior; for they had certain intelligence that the Elector of Brandenburg, dissatisfied with the states on account of the inheritance of King William's estates, would not be over-hasty in sending his troops to the rendezvous; and that the Danes, who were at Nimeguen, had refused to march, by reason of the arrears due to them. Upon this advice, Marshal Villeroy wrote to the elector, to invite him to share the victory, which he flattered himself he was upon the point of gaining.

The states getting intelligence of the contents of this letter, wrote to the Danes to join the army with all possible expedition, and they would give them immediate satisfaction. They readily obeyed, and their generals being advised of the design of the French, hastened the march of the Wirtemberg troops; and, after taking proper measures, it was resolved rather to attack than wait the enemy. The French, who were advanced as far as Ramillies, seeing us, contrary to their expectations, on our march, were terribly embarrassed, and imagined they had received false intelligence; however, there was no avoiding a battle.

We began on the 23rd, about two in the afternoon. The left of our army, which attacked the right wing of the enemy, met with a stout resistance before they could break them; which, however, they at length did, and put them to flight, while we were not less successful in the right wing. In a word, the enemy was everywhere entirely routed, and never victory was more complete. The shattered remains of their army fled in the greatest confusion, some to Louvain, others to Waveren, and the rest to Judoigne. We took a great number of prisoners in the pursuit, many colours and standards; artillery and ammunition, tin pontons and baggage. I escaped unhurt, though in the hottest of the battle, till the French were entirely defeated; when an unlucky shell from a steeple, on which, before the battle, they had planted some mortars and cannon, which played all the time of the engagement, struck the back part of my head, and fractured my skull.

I was carried to Meldre, or Meldert, a small town in the quarter of Louvain, two leagues south-east from that university, and five leagues north-west from Ramillies, upon a small brook which washes Tirlemont. I was here trepanned, and great care taken of me, but I did not recover in less than ten weeks. Though I suffered great torture by this wound, yet the discovery it caused of my sex, in the fixing of my dressing, by which the surgeons saw my breasts, and, by the largeness of my nipples, concluded I had given suck, was a greater grief to me. No sooner had they made this discovery, but they acquainted Brigadier Preston, that his pretty dragoon (so I was always called) was, in fact, a woman. He was very loath to believe it, and did me the honour to say, he had always looked upon me as the prettiest fellow, and the best man he had. His incredulity made him send for my brother, whom he now imagined to be my husband; when he came, the brigadier said to him, 'Dick, I am surprised at a piece of news these gentlemen tell me; they say, your brother is, in reality, a woman.'

'Sir,' said he, 'since she is discovered, I cannot deny it; she is my wife, and I have had three children by her.'

The news of this discovery spread far and near, and reaching, among others, my Lord John Hay's ear, he came to see me, as did all my former comrades. My lord would neither ask me, nor suffer any one else, any questions; but called for my husband, though first for my comrade, who had been long my bedfellow, and examined him closely. The fellow protested, as it was truth, that he never knew I was a woman, or even suspected it; It is well known, continued he, that she had a child lain to her, and took care of it. My lord then calling in my husband, desired him to tell the meaning of my disguise.

He gave him a full and satisfactory account of our first acquaintance, marriage, and situation, with the manner of his having entered into the service, and my resolution to go in search of him; adding the particulars of our meeting, and my obstinate refusal of bedding with him. My lord seemed very well entertained with my history, and ordered that I should want for nothing, and that my pay should be continued while under cure. When his lordship heard that I was well enough recovered to go abroad, he generously sent me a parcel of shirts and sheets to make me shifts. Brigadier Preston made me a present of a handsome silk gown; every one of our officers contributed to the furnishing me with what was requisite for the dress of my sex, and dismissed me the service with a handsome compliment.

I being thus equipped, waited on my lord, the brigadier, and other my benefactors, to return them thanks for the obligations they had lain me under. My lord said, he hoped I would not continue my cruelty to my husband, now that I could no longer pass under a disguise. I answered. My lord, I must own, I have a strong inclination to the army, and I apprehended the consequence of conversing with my husband might be my dismission; for a great belly could not have been concealed. The discovery of my sex has now removed the cause, and I have no objection to living with my husband, as it is the duty of an honest wife.

'Well,' said my lord, 'I am satisfied with your reason, and we will have a new marriage.' Accordingly all our officers were invited, and we were, with great solemnity, wedded and bedded; the sack-posset eaten, and the stocking thrown. After this ceremony, every one, at taking leave, would kiss the bride, and left me a piece of gold, some four or five, to put me in a way of life.

I conceived the first night, having never known man, except my husband, but the time I was surprised, as I have before related. An idle life was what I could never away with; beside, I was under a necessity, having now no pay, to do something for a support; wherefore I undertook to cook for our regiment, returning to my husband's quarters every night. I did not long carry on this business, as the close attendance it required prevented my marauding, which was vastly more beneficial. After I had given over my cooking, I turned sutler, and, by the indulgence of the officers, was permitted to pitch my tent in the front, while others were driven to the rear of the army.

The rapidity of the conquests which attended the victory of Ramillies, is so remarkable, that it would be unpardonable in me to pass it over in silence to continue my particular history.

Our victorious army having rested the night which followed the battle, briskly pursued the enemy the next morning; drew near to

Judoigne, and crossed the Dyle on the 25th, near Louvain. This large city, being abandoned, submitted; we took possession of all the great stores of all sorts of provisions, which I have already said the enemy had there lain up, and placed a garrison in it. From hence our army marched on to Brussels; from which town the Elector of Bavaria, and his court, had retired after the last battle, in which he shared no laurels with the marshal, as he had hoped: wherefore, the town being summoned by a letter from the Duke of Marlborough and the deputies of the states, opened her gates and submitted to King Charles. Malines, or Mechlin, followed this example, as did Lire, situated on the Nethe, and strongly fortified.

The Elector of Bavaria, who had no settled place since his and the marshal's defeat, seemed determined to stand the allies behind the Scheld, near Ghent, with the troops he had saved; but they did not give him time to intrench himself, for they decamped from Grimbergen on the 30th, passed by Alost, and being advanced as far as Meerbeek, they heard that the enemy had abandoned the lines in Flanders, and retired behind their old lines, near Merien and Courtray. While the army was on their march, I joined it, being entirely recovered. On this advice, Ghent was summoned, which surrendered to Major-General Cadogan, on condition that their privileges should be preserved. General Fagel possessed himself of Bruges, on the same terms; and, without striking a stroke, made himself master of Dam, a small, but a very strong town, and of the castle of Rodenhuis, or Red-house,

After the enemy had abandoned all their lines in the country of Waas, the garrison of Antwerp making a show of defence, general Cadogan marched thither with twelve hundred men, and summoned the place. After many parleys, it was at last agreed that the garrison should march out on the 7th of June, with arms and baggage, drums beating, colours flying, four mortars, and as many cannon. The next day the French also evacuated Fort Pearl, Fort Mary, and Fort Philip, situated on the Scheld, and near to Antwerp. Even Oudenard, a strong fortified town on the same river, between four and five leagues distant from. Ghent, being summoned on the 1st of June, surrendered on composition the next day, the Marquis de Bournonville seeing four pieces of cannon mounted on a battery. Thus the winning of one single battle reduced in a few days, all Brabant, and a great part of Flanders, to the obedience of King Charles.

That the fruit of such a successful opening of a campaign might not be lost, the Duke of Marlborough, went to the Hague, to consult the states-general on the plan of military expeditions, and returned to the camp on the 13th of June, when he immediately invested Ostend by land, while Admiral Fairborn blocked it up by sea with nine men-of-war, and four bomb-*ketches*. We could not entirely enclose the town, without taking Fort de Plasendaal, raised on the canal of Bruges; General Fagel attacked this with such resolution, that the garrison, consisting of two hundred and fifty men, was made prisoners of war. The fire upon the town, both from the land and sea, was so terrible, that it capitulated on the 6th of July; she had, under the government of the Archduke Albert, held out a three years' siege, and now hardly so many days. The garrison was suffered to march out with their swords, and them only on condition that they should not, of six months, bear arms against King Charles, or his allies.

After the reduction of Ostend, our army encamped with the right at Wellem, the left at Harlebeck. Hither the town of Courtray sent deputies to the generals to make its submission, the French having abandoned it after having exacted large contributions. Brigadier Meredith went to blockade, and try if he could reduce it by famine, while the grand army undertook the siege of Menin, with two hundred pieces of cannon, great and small, brought from. Maestricht and Holland. General Salisch, who had the direction of this important siege, invested the place the 22nd of July; which, though called the key of France, held out but eighteen days after our trenches were opened, and surrendered upon terms in a month after it was invested.

We lost a great many men in this siege; I was myself exposed to no danger but when my husband was, whom I always followed, and whom I would never abandon, wherever he went. While the army stayed here to fill up the works, and repair the breaches, General Churchill was detached with six battalions, and the same number of squadrons, to reduce Dendermond, which made a more obstinate resistance than was expected. The general acquitted himself so well of his commission, that this town, which was almost inaccessible, surrendered on the 5th of September.

The siege of Ath was next undertaken, by Field-Marshal Ouwerkerke, or Auverquerque, with forty battalions and thirty squadrons. General Ingoldsby broke ground on the 20th, at night, with the loss of one man only; for, the enemy imagining we should open our trenches on the side where the Lord Auverquerque was, had drawn their strength to that quarter, to prevent, or impede, his works. Our men covered themselves before they discovered their mistake. When my husband marched with General Ingoldsby to the side where they were to break ground, he left me boiling the pot, with which I designed to regale him and the officers of his regiment. When my meat was ready, I covered it with cloths so close that no steam could get out, and, venturing through a village belonging to the enemy, in which I ran the hazard of being killed or stripped, by a circuit of five miles, I got safe, with my provisions on my head, to the trench. It was a fatiguing journey, the way being difficult to find, and the night being very dark: but what danger will deter a woman who truly loves her husband? having found mine, I set my broth and meat before him; he invited his colonel, and other officers, who were not a little surprised at the risk I had run, and that I could bring it so hot such a length of way.

Lord Auverquerque, who was come to thank the officers and soldiers for their diligence, stood talking to some of the former, when I, looking through the sand-bags, saw a soldier, who, ignorant of our being on the side we were, came out of the town to gather turnips. I took a piece out of one of our people's hand, and called to an officer to see me shoot him; for we had pushed our trenches within thirty-three paces of the palisades. I suppose we were just then perceived; for the instant I killed the man, a musket-shot, from the town, came through the sand-bags, split my under lip, beat one of my teeth into my mouth, and knocked me down. Both this shot and mine, with which I killed the soldier, were so exactly at a time, that none could distinguish whether I fell by the recoiling of the piece, or the enemy's ball. My husband, and some of his comrades, ran to take me up, and seeing me bloody, imagined I was shot through the head; but I convinced them to the contrary, by spitting the ball and tooth into my hand.

General Ingoldsby sent for his surgeon, who sewed up my lip, and took care of me in the cure. Lord Auverquerque, who had seen what had passed, made me a present of five *pistoles*, and told me, he was sorry that the pains I had taken, in providing refreshment for my husband and his officers, had been attended with such a misfortune. I stayed in the trench till the next night, when our regiment, for so I call that of my husband, being relieved by another, marched off. In a few days the breaches were so wide, that the besieged beat the chamade in the afternoon of the 30th of September, but all terms were refused them, and the garrison, consisting of two thousand one hundred men, on the 2nd of October, were obliged to surrender prisoners of war: the officers, however, were allowed their swords and baggage.

The reduction of this town put an end to the campaign of 1706, In the Low Countries. We joined the grand army, which, under the Duke of Marlborough, covered the siege, and, in a fortnight after, moved to St. Quintin-Lennick, in order to separate, and march into winter-quarters. Our regiment was quartered in Ghent, where I was delivered of a child before my time, which lived about half a year. Rather than live upon the spend, an idle life, I hired myself to Mr. Dupper, who, since, kept a tavern on Fish-street-hill, and was then head sutler, to be under the cook. While I was in this service, the cook had one day orders to dress something for Mr. Stone the surgeon, which was ready for the table, when lieutenant St. Leger, of General Evans's regiment of foot, came into the kitchen, and would have it for himself; the cook would not yield to it, and the lieutenant knocked him down; I was then in my back kitchen washing my dishes, and seeing the brutality of the action, it raised my spirits, I ran to the lieutenant, collared him, threw up his heels, and, in the fall, he broke his leg.

Mr. Dupper, Mr. Stone, and several others ran in to know the grounds of this scuffle, which, upon hearing, everyone allowed me to have been in the right. Mr. Stone refused to set his leg, which was done by a French surgeon, but after such a bungling manner, that it was an eyesore to his dying day; no small mortification to him, who was a tall, strong, well-made, black man, had a very handsome face, and a genteel, easy shape; all which, he needed nobody to tell him, for he had no small opinion of himself. He was descended from Sir Anthony St. Leger, who possessed an estate, as I have heard, of ten thousand a year in Kent, which he very much impaired in the service of King Charles I., whose cause he strenuously asserted against his rebellious subjects.

This lieutenant was not a little proud of his family, though I have heard among the officers, what ground they had for it I can't say, that his father was but a merry-begotten son of Sir Anthony's; but this, others have contradicted, and given for reason, that King Charles II. put our lieutenant's father and brother into the Charterhouse. The gentleman I am speaking of, was haughty, morose, and vain: I believe he did not want courage, notwithstanding he was very much of the bully, a gamester, a known setter, and a sharper at play. His misfortune became a standing jest; for whenever he was quarrelsome in company, he was menaced with me. Some years after, I met him in the Tilt-yard coffee-house, where a gentleman asked him if he knew me; he answered, he had seen my face somewhere. 'Why,' said the other, 'have you forgot Kit Welsh, who broke your leg?'

He then looked more earnestly at me, but said no more than, 'D—n her, she is strangely altered, she is grown fat.'

''Tis true,' said I, 'in my person I am altered, but not in my temper; for, should I see you knock down, as you did, a man of much inferior strength, as was our cook, I might, perhaps, give you another broken leg:' he returned me some curses, which he could do as well as any officer in the army, (for he swore a round hand,) and left the coffee-house.

During my stay in Ghent, the Dutch woman with whom I found my husband at Breda, whom he had promised never more to see, the condition on which I forgave his lubricity, had the confidence to take a lodging opposite to ours, and one day, just when I had prepared dinner, inveigled him to an alehouse. I knew not where he was, and being impatient, went out to look him, and was informed by a neighbour, that he was at such an alehouse with his mistress. This news setting me in a flame, I ran directly thither, and saw them sitting in a box, the woman outermost. My rage was so great, that I struck at her with a case-knife I had undesignedly brought out in my hand, and cut her nose off close to the face, except a small part of the skin, by which it hung.

My husband leaping over the table, ran to the mainguard for a surgeon, who sewed it on again; but the wound, however, disfigured her, and I ran for an officer to secure them both. My husband, by order of the colonel, was confined, and reprimanded very severely, and, had I not interposed when my passion was over, he had been made run the gantelope: as he was confined during my pleasure, I was no sooner cool, but I procured his liberty. His *dulcinea* did not come off at as easy a rate, for she was put into a turning-stool, and whirled round till she was dizzy, and so sick that she emptied her stomach. This stool is like a round cage, big enough to hold one person, fixed upon a spindle, and being only railed in, the criminal is exposed to the ridicule of all the bystanders.

After she had undergone this punishment, she was, with great ceremony, conducted out of the gates of the town. I own the violence of my temper, which is a very jealous one, pushed me on too far in this business, for I am satisfied, in the place where I found them, they could not wrong me; and, indeed, I have reason to believe my husband never injured me with women from the time I found him. To say the truth, I can tax his memory with nothing but an unhappy itch to play, which he could not be broke of, though it almost broke me, and was the only cause of uneasiness that I ever had all the time I was his wife. The woman who raised my jealousy, married at Groningen; I often afterwards met her, and was as well pleased, as she was mortified, at the figure she made by the amputation of her nose, and its being stitched on again.

Soon after my rough treatment of my husband's quondam mistress, a man and a woman were executed for a barbarous murder. He was married to a very handsome woman at Oudenard, by whom he had had three children, and she was, at the time he perpetrated this villainy, big of the fourth. The female criminal was his servant, a very pretty girl, but not to be put in competition with his wife, though he gave her the preference. He carried on an intrigue with this wench, and that he might do it without control, resolved to take his wife off by poison, which he accordingly prepared, and bade the wench put it into her mistress's water-gruel, then went to Ghent.

She punctually performed this order, and it had the dire effect proposed: the poor woman swelled amazingly, and was in the utmost torture; her little boy, about nine years old, hearing his mother cry out in her agonies, ran and brought her relations; but no remedy could relieve her, and it being evident that she was poisoned, the maid was secured, who, in prison, to excuse herself, said she had put something into her mistress's water-gruel, which was given her by her master to that end. Upon this confession, four men, one of which was the unhappy wife's brother, were appointed to watch his return to the town, which was about sunset. He was immediately seized, and clapped into a separate prison, and, in few days, the whole truth was sifted out; on which they were condemned, and the next day executed; the maid was beheaded, and the master broke upon the wheel. The execution over, they were hung up in iron chains, the woman by the heels, the man by the neck.

As this year, 1706, was remarkable for the memorable march of Prince Eugene to, and raising the siege of Turin, I believe I shall not displease my readers by taking a step into Italy, and giving a short account of the situation of affairs in Savoy; where the French had spoiled that duke of the greater part of his country. On the 29th of September they invested Turin, but the court of Versailles being of opinion that their troops in Piedmont were not sufficient, they withdrew from thence on the 10th of October, and attempted Asti; but failing there, they made themselves amends by the reduction of Nice, which the duke of Berwick invested the 31st of October, and took by capitulation on the 4th of January of this year.

During the winter, 1705, the King of France had made such preparations for the reduction of the capital of Savoy, as were amazing, and
gave everyone ground to believe his success infallible. The duke, on
the other hand, notwithstanding the French had possessed themselves
of so many of his towns, did not lose courage, but did everything that
a brave and prudent prince ought for the defence of his country; employing the subsidies he drew from England and Holland, in well stor-
ing his metropolis with provision and ammunition, in repairing the
old, and adding new fortifications. The town being invested about the
middle of May, was assaulted and defended with equal and surprising
bravery, though with different success on either side.

While, at Turin, they were furiously intent upon the taking and
retaking the outworks, Prince Eugene began his march for Italy with
the imperial army, greatly re-enforced by the auxiliary troops of England and Holland. All that the Duke of Vendome could do to impede his inarch, proved fruitless; he broke through all the obstacles
the French threw in his way, and subsisted his army in the midst of an
enemy's country, which he was obliged to cross; passed several large
rivers, and, in thirty-four marches, joined the duke of Savoy on the 1st
of September, within four leagues of Turin.

The extremity to which this city was reduced, hastening their
preparations, the army crossed the Doria on the 6th, with design to
attack the enemy the next morning, as they did, marching up to the
trench, reserving their own, and receiving their fire at the very foot
of their intrenchments, where they fell upon them with such fury,
and so close and terrible a fire, that nothing could withstand them.
The French, driven from trench to trench, and pursued with a cruel
slaughter, abandoned all their artillery and ammunition, and sought
their safety in their flight. This glorious victory not only delivered the
capital, but retrieved what the duke had lost, and was followed by the
submission of the Milanese to King Charles III.

We are now come to the year 1707, in which Marshal Villars forced
the lines of Stolhossen, on the Upper Rhine, got a considerable booty,
took two hundred pieces of cannon, opened himself a passage into
Germany, and exacted contribution on all hands. The consternation
this caused, made the court of Vienna strenuously solicit the States-
general and the electors, to send immediate succours for the defence
of the empire, and offer the command of the imperial army, as *generalissimo*, to the elector of Hanover, the late King George, who accepted

it at the solicitation of Queen Anne and the states-general; but nothing more was done on the Upper Rhine this campaign, than observing the motions of one another.

The Duke of Marlborough arrived at the Hague on the 12th of May, and from thence, without loss of time, he set out for the army encamped at Lembeek. The attention of all being turned on the siege of Toulon, where the allies miscarried, nothing of importance was done this campaign in the Low Countries; wherefore, as the Battle of Almanza was fought this year, my reader will forgive me if I turn his eyes upon Spain, where the allies having raised the siege of Barcelona, penetrated as far as Madrid, which King Philip abandoned and went to head the succours sent him by France, as he declared in his manifesto: which succours were so considerable, that, being joined with the troops that had been compelled to raise the siege of Barcelona, and had marched through Navarre into Castile, his army was stronger than that of the allies by twenty-five squadrons and thirteen battalions, besides the inhabitants of the country, who had taken up arms in his cause.

Wherefore the allies seeing that King Charles continued still in Aragon, thought proper to quit this capital in their turn. King Charles at length joined the army on the 8th of August, with two regiments of horse and three battalions; but it was too late, they had let slip the opportunity, and the best they could now do, was to march to the frontiers of Valencia and Murcia, and so to distribute the winter-quarters as to be able to cover those two kingdoms, with Aragon and Catalonia. King Charles, with a few troops, withdrew to Barcelona; and on his retreat, the French took in a great number of towns, castles, and forts, which had deserted from King Philip upon the raising the siege of Barcelona. In the spring, it was resolved in a council held in Valencia, to assemble in one body all the troops, and by the way of Aragon to penetrate into Castile, and destroy the magazines which the enemy had made on the frontiers.

The whole army took the field on the 6th of April, to put the project in execution. The number of the allies were fifty-three squadrons and forty-two battalions, which having destroyed the enemy's magazines at Baudera, Yela, and Montalegre, they besieged the castle of Villena; but before any breach made, the enemy, having, near Almanza, formed a body of seventy-six squadrons, and fifty-four battalions, were preparing to march, and join seven or eight thousand French under the command of the Duke of Orleans. As the allies did not imagine

72

the enemy so strong, it was resolved, in a council of war held the 24th, to attack them before their proposed junction; accordingly they began their march the next morning, and about noon, coming on the plain in sight of the enemy, these latter raised their piquet, and ranged in order of battle before the town of Almanza.

The English and Dutch, who began the fight, notwithstanding they behaved with as much bravery as men could do, were twice repulsed, and the enemy obtained a complete victory. About three thousand were taken prisoners; the better part of the foot was cut to pieces, and the few that remained passed the Ebro under the conduct of Lord Galway and the Marquis de las Minas. The havoc made of the allies had been much greater, and possibly no quarters had been given, if the Duke of Berwick had not interposed.

After this signal victory, the conquerors found no difficulty to make themselves masters of Requina, and of almost all the kingdom of Valencia; and dividing their army into three corps, that under the Duke of Orleans took in Calatajud, and on the 25th of May appeared before Saragossa. The garrison the allies left there, withdrew the night before into Catalonia, so that the town came to the best terms they could with the duke, who put into it two thousand men. The Chevalier d'Asfeld, who commanded the second corps, after having taken Xativa sword in hand, left the castle invested, to join the troops which the Bishop of Murcia had set on foot, and to besiege Alicant.

In the interim, the Earl of Galway, having drawn out the garrisons of several places, had taken post behind the Segre, and, to maintain it, began to raise trenches and redoubts from Tortosa even. beyond Lerida, but the Duke of Berwick, with a third body, having joined the duke of Orleans, it was resolved, notwithstanding the excessive heats, to dislodge the English generals, to cross the Ebro, and to penetrate into Catalonia. The cannon being arrived, they placed it on the bank of the Cinca; made so strong a fire upon four squadrons posted on the other side, that they were obliged to retire: after which the enemy crossed the river, and Fraga having been abandoned by the garrison, they had no obstacle to hinder them from besieging Lerida.

The fortifications of this place were in fine repair; and three thousand English, who were in garrison, had had the precaution to destroy the houses, gardens, and trees, that were in the neighbourhood. The violent heats being over, the Duke of Orleans sent his foot before, on the 10th of September, and followed them with the horse a few days after; but they spent near a month in making preparations for the siege: the trenches were not opened till the 2nd of October.

Notwithstanding the besieged made a gallant defence, the assailants pushed forward their works. On the 12th the breach was large enough to attack the covered way, where the besiegers made a lodgement, after an obstinate and bloody dispute of two full hours. This obliged the garrison to retire to the castle, before which the trenches were opened on the 16th, at night, though it was opposed by some general officers, who opined for a blockade, because the season was far advanced, and that the earl of Galway was on his march to succour the besieged: but the precaution taken to guard all the passes, rendered his attempt fruitless. The Duke of Orleans having carried the outworks sword in hand the 1st of November, made several mines, and battered the main body of the place. The garrison being thus straitened, capitulated on the 10th, and was allowed all military honours, and to be conducted to Lord Galway the nearest way; besides, a free pardon was granted to the inhabitants.

The siege of Ciudad Rodrigo, in the kingdom of Leon, was next undertaken, and taken on capitulation. The winter drawing on, the Spaniards not having provided what was necessary for new enterprises, nothing more was done in Catalonia this campaign. In Flanders, as I have before said, the French and allies were in a manner inactive; though the former was, at home, secretly employed in preparing for the execution of a project, which had it succeeded, would have quite disconcerted the latter, and have made Lewis XIV. triumph for all his enemies; but as secret as were his preparations, they were discovered by the Dutch, who gave the queen of England advice by a fishing-boat, that the design was formed, and everything in readiness to make a descent on some part of her dominions in favour of the Pretender.

The event proved, that the states-general were not imposed upon in the intelligence they had received; for the French embarked twelve battalions on board a sufficient number of ships, with everything necessary; some thousands of spare arms, and four millions of *livres*. On the 5th of March, 1708, the king went to St. Germains to take his leave of the Pretender, and, in wishing him a happy issue, made him a present of a sword set with diamonds, worth fifty thousand *livres*, desiring him to remember that it was a French sword. Having made a suitable compliment to the king, the Pretender took his leave of the dauphin and the other princes of the blood, and that very day set out for Dunkirk, from whence he set sail the 17th, at night, with a number of volunteers, big with the hopes of being joined by such malcontents in Scotland, where he designed to land, as were averse to the union, and with the troops which followed, and the assistance of such Scots, to submit the whole kingdom of Great Britain.

The designs of France being timely discovered, the English and states-general soon got ready a fleet of forty men-of-war under the command of the late Lord Torrington, who, with all the sail they could crowd, followed the French, having advice of their departure and course. In the mean while some English troops drawn out of the garrisons of Flanders, were sent to England by the way of Ostend. The Pretender came to an anchor near Edinburgh; fired the number of cannon agreed upon with his partisans; and hoped the signal would raise some thousands of malcontents, who would take arms to support his pretensions. On the certain assurances made him of an insurrection, preparations were making to disembark his troops, but the English, by a great deal an over-match for the French, appearing in sight, suspended the landing.

A council was held, in which it was resolved to send three ships close to the town to land their troops in case they perceived any commotion in their favour; but these having the mortification to find none moved, but to repel them in the attempt, they were obliged to drop the enterprise, and make the best of their way to the coast of France. They were chased by the English, and the Salisbury taken. Thus the Pretender returned to Dunkirk the beginning of April, and all his hopes were dissipated like smoke; the unsuccessful project only served to irritate the allies against France, and brought them to a resolution of acting with more vigour than they had yet done. To this end the Duke of Marlborough, who had made a tour into Germany, set out for Brabant on the 3rd of May, and before the end of the month had drawn the army together. The French also, on their side, assembled their forces, and the Dukes of Burgundy and Berry, who were to command this year, accompanied by the Pretender and Count Thoulouse, arrived at the camp.

After many motions, the allies encamped near Louvain, the French at Genap and Braine la Leuze; both armies intrenching as if they designed to try which would be first weary of staying; but on a sudden, when none expected it, the French, on the 4th of July, at night, sent away sixteen thousand men, who marched by the way of Enghien to Alost, and broke all the bridges behind them on the Dender. The body of their army coming to Halle, orders were sent to the above detachment to march with all speed to Ninove, and from thence the following night to Ghent, each horseman with a foot soldier behind him; they arrived as the gates were opening, and having forced the guard of *burghers*, made themselves masters of the town; upon which, the garrison, not being strong enough to make any defence, immediately capitulated.

At the same time the Count de la Motte, who was in Walloon Flanders, marching with a body of thirteen thousand men, and some pieces of cannon, to Bruges, found the town unprovided with troops, and seized upon it on the 6th of this same month; after which, he carried Fort Plassendal sword in hand.

At the first intelligence of the march of the French, the allies pursued them with all possible expedition, and even fell upon their rearguard, but could not prevent their continuing their march; wherefore, on advice of the Joss of these three places, they marched with all speed towards Oudenard, to meet with the enemy, between the Scheld and the Lis, on their return to the frontiers of France, and force them to a battle. To this end Monsieur Rantzau and general Cadogan were detached to secure the pass of Lessines, while the army bent its march the same way. On the 11th, about noon, these officers discovered the French army intrenched below Oudenard, on a ground encumbered with hedges and bushes. They immediately gave notice of it to the grand army, and had orders sent back to attack them without losing a minute's time. They accordingly charged them at the village, whence they drove them with great slaughter.

The rest of the army having passed the Scheld, formed themselves as they advanced, and began the fight about four o'clock, with a great deal of resolution, but the foot only engaged, the hedges and hollow ways hindering the horse from coming in for any share in the action. The French were driven from hedge to hedge, and everywhere trodden under foot; however, they behaved very gallantly, and disputed every inch of ground, till, being taken in the rear by eighteen battalions and some horse, they began to lose courage, quitted the field, where they left a great number of their dead, and taking advantage of the darkness of the night, fled in great disorder, and sheltered themselves under the cannon of Ghent.

We could not have obtained a more complete victory. We soon after moved to Courtray; there, Colonel Cholmondeley's men, who lay without the town, near the palisades, were drawn up to be reviewed by their officers, while I was going into the town to purchase provisions for my tent. The colonel, who was of a gay, lively temper, and pretty much of what we call the wag, seeing me go into the town, waited for my coming out, that he might divert himself by teasing me, which he did not a little delight in. I carried my provisions on a mare; the colonel had a small black stone-horse, which, when he saw me returning, he turned loose, and the horse, like a brute as he was, began to be very rude with my poor beast, and in his rough courtship broke me four bottles of wine.

I was so irritated at this, that having driven away his unmannerly tit, I pursued the colonel with stones, but he eluded my anger by his flight, and told the officers, that his stone-horse had an amour with Kit Welsh. Sometime after this, as I was upon my mare, in a dress convenient for my vocation. Mr. Montgomery, captain of the grenadiers in Lord Orkney's regiment, began to ridicule my habit, and make a jest of my poor beast. I offered to run her against his horse for a *pistole*, and we would both ride. Brigadier Godfrey, who was by, laid another *pistole* on my side. We both went to the place chosen to run upon, and starting at the beat of drum, placed to give the signal, he suffered me to keep pace with him some time, but finding he was going to leave me, I made a furious push at him, flung man and horse into a ditch, and thus won the race. The brigadier laughed heartily at my stratagem, the captain was half angry, but I got a couple of *pistoles*, (for the brigadier gave me that he had won,) and did not much concern myself, nor should I have given myself any trouble had he been irritated, for I may safely say, I had as little fear about me as any man in the army.

The allies having received a re-enforcement of German troops which had followed Prince Eugene from the Moselle to the Low Countries, possessed themselves of the lines the French had thrown up to cover Walloon Flanders; extended their contributions as far as the gates of Arras, and made preparations to lay siege to Lisle. As soon as the heavy cannon and a convoy of five thousand waggons laden with provision and ammunition, which Prince Eugene himself escorted with a body of forty thousand men, were arrived, the town was invested on the 1st of August. It was abundantly supplied with everything necessary to hold out a long siege; and Marshal Boufflers, who commanded in it, had with him ten thousand, some said thirteen thousand men.

The trenches were opened the 11th, at night, and the works were carried on without intermission, while the Grand Army observed that of the French, which was daily re-enforced: for as the siege employed the whole strength of the allies, they could safely disgarnish most of their towns; besides which they received a strong re-enforcement led by the duke of Berwick out of Germany; so that their army consisted of a hundred and twenty-six battalions and two hundred and eight squadrons. With these considerable forces, they marched by the way of Orchies, Bergues, and Pevele towards Phalempin, and having taken out of Douay thirty pieces of heavy cannon, they drew near the allies the 5th of September, whom, though re-enforced the night before by a detachment of seventy-seven squadrons from the army carrying on the siege, everyone expected they would attack: but the Duke of Marlborough soon discovering that they designed only to retard the siege, ordered the tents to be pitched, fortified his camp with the utmost care, and sent back to the siege a part of the troops he had received from thence.

In the interim of these motions, the besiegers having pushed as far as the glacis of the counterscarp, four thousand grenadiers, beside those who were employed in the works, were commanded to give the assault, which began at night on the 9th of September, and a most furious one it was. The enemies' fire from their outworks, which were not yet demolished, made a dismal havoc, and certainly this was the most bloody action that ever was seen: the assailants, notwithstanding, made several lodgements on the covered way, spite of the gallant resistance of the besieged.

There were some English and Dutch troops posted in the market-town called Entrieres, where they had intrenched themselves: these the duke of Vendome cannonaded with forty pieces of cannon, which made us all conclude he would at length come to a battle: but he, secretly decamping on the 15th, lined the Scheld from Tournay to Ghent, and the canal from thence to Bruges; by which he cut off all the convoys the allies might have had from the frontier towns, except from Ostend. Eight thousand English were landed at this port, with a great quantity of powder and provision, and stores of all sorts, a great part of which had already been received by the besiegers.

As the remainder was still considerable, and was every day increasing by fresh supplies from England, Major-General Webb and Count Nassau-Woudenburg were detached with thirty battalions to escort it; my husband was in this detachment, whom I followed, and the Duke of Marlborough advanced beyond Menin, almost as far as Marquette, to be at hand to sustain us. We were joined by a second detachment of twelve battalions and twenty-eight squadrons, and met the convoy at Hoogleden, where we had advice that Monsieur la Motte was marching with a body of twenty-three thousand men and better, to attack it near Wenendal; upon which news our men were immediately formed into two lines, at the issue of the defile near the castle of Wenendal, and our generals posted, on each side, a regiment in the coppice with orders to lie snug, and not to fire till they were sure of taking the enemy in flank.

Hardly was this disposition made before the enemy appeared in sight. They formed the infantry into four lines, and the horse in as many, and entered the defile to attack the escort: but they were no sooner within our ambush but they were saluted with a general discharge on either hand, which put their right and left into a thorough disorder; they, however, formed again very soon, and even made two battalions give way a little, but Albemarle's regiment coming up to oppose their passage directly in their fronts kept them in play, and gave time to make some fresh troops advance. Seeing themselves attacked in front, and open on the flanks to an incessant fire, the two wings were forced in disorder up their centre, and all of them returning the way they had come, hastened out of the defile, where they left four thousand of their dead, and some pieces of cannon.

The French general not being able to lead on his third attack, was obliged to retreat, and suffer the convoy to pass. We had not above six or seven thousand men, so that they were above three to one. The conduct of General Webb greatly contributed to this victory, which, however, he paid dear for by the wounds he received. I got a fine bay horse with silver-capped pistols and laced housings and pistol-bags. I sold my horse to Colonel Hamilton for nine *pistoles*; my pistols to Captain Brown for five crowns; and the lace of my furniture, excepting what I reserved to lace the knees of my husband's breeches, to a Jew, at five *livres* an ounce.

The safe arrival of this convoy, was a subject of great joy to the allies, who must have raised the siege had it miscarried. As they began to want powder in the town, notwithstanding the care that was taken to store it with all necessaries in abundance, the French endeavoured to supply them with a good number of bags, which their horse carried behind them. This enterprise was undertaken the very night after the Battle of Wenendal. A detachment was made of three small bodies of horse, with green boughs in their hats, which was the distinction of our troops: the first party succeeded in this stratagem, and calling themselves Germans, had the good fortune to get into the town; the second, being discovered, were all blown up, by our fire taking their powder, or made prisoners; and the third returned back the way they were coming.

The besiegers having, though with the loss of a great many brave fellows, made their way, on the 3rd of October attacked the half-moon at noonday: they carried the work, but before they could lodge themselves, the fire from the town killed two hundred and fifty of their men; they kept the post notwithstanding. The siege was carried on with such resolution, that on the 22nd the governor found himself under a necessity of hanging out a white ensign. The town, after the capitulations were signed, was surrendered to the allies. Seventeen hundred French horse were conducted to Douay. The rest of the garrison, which was six thousand men, retired into the citadel, which was surrounded with a double ditch and a number of outworks.

During this siege, which was not more bravely attacked than defended, as I was one day a foraging, I entered a *chateau*, deserted by the enemy, and found in it a basket of eggs, and another of cocks and hens, (in the camp language, corporals and their wives,) which I made free with; the eggs I presented to the Duke of Argyle, and the fowls to some officers. The next day I returned to the same place, and got corn, hay, and straw, for my mare. The third visit I made with a resolution to search more narrowly, for something of greater consequence, but some of our men had been there, and deceived my hopes; for I could meet with nothing more valuable than what I had before carried off; therefore I was forced to content myself with provender for my mare.

In the time I was searching, some of the French army came in upon me, and took both myself, my mare, and my forage. The soldiers were quarrelling about the right to my clothes when their officer came in, whom by good fortune I knew. He asked me, what had brought me thither, and who I was. I answered, that I thought he ought to know me, being a son of Captain Maclaughings of Clare's regiment; (for I was in man's clothes;) 'Well now, honey,' said he, 'I vawsh not after knowing you before, but give my humble service to my cushin and naamshake; but heark'ye now, joy, are you Richard or John?'

'Fait,' said I, in the brogue, 'I am Richard'

'Well now, cushin,' replied he, 'what will I do for you; but indeed, honey, nobody shall meddle wid your tings, joy, but go in te name of Cott.'

I made the best of my way to the Duke of Argyle's quarters, where I found his grace and the Lord Mark Kerr at chess. I asked them with some warmth, in a language which only became a soldier, and a freedom allowed my sex, what they meant by having no better intelligence, and idling their time at chess while the French were on the point of cannonading us. I had, in returning from my *chateau*, observed all the hedges lined and the cannon ready to play upon us. The Lord Mark Kerr, surprised to see his grace pay any regard to what I had said, told him, I was a foolish drunken woman, and not worth notice: to which the duke replied, he would as soon take my advice as that of any brigadier in the army. He then asked me my reasons; I told him, and had hardly done it, when he found my intelligence true, and that we had scarce time to get into the lines for safety.

Sir Richard Temple's and How's regiments were ordered to clear the hedges, and the duke would have gone with them, and probably never returned, had I not prevented him by keeping back his horse; for both these regiments were cut to pieces before our horse and train of artillery came up, which soon drove them to the main body of their army. The enemy cannonaded the Duke of Argyle's quarters so soon, that there was no making a bed for him there; and he was obliged to take up with one of straw of my making, and Colonel Campbell for a chum. They had no candles, but I had two of wax taken out of a priest's house, and hung up one over their heads in a paper lantern.

Here they slept very comfortably, and I took the opportunity to steal the duke's wine for the poor fellows upon the guard, who I thought wanted it to comfort them: I had left but two bottles, which occasioned the duke's butler making a great uproar. In the morning his grace gave me a *pistole* for my early intelligence, and at night I spent it on two of his servants, at a house of civil conversation, where one of them was received with so warm an affection, that he must be ungrateful if he ever forgets it, for the favour she bestowed on him was of a lasting sort. I don't care to mention his name, but he was coachman to the Duke of Roxburgh within this century.

At the siege of the city, Taylor the corporal, whose eye I struck out in defence of my pig, having received the company's money, instead of paying them, lost it at play, and then desperately shot himself through the head.

The 5th day after the reduction of Lisle, Lord Auverquerque died; he was field-marshal of the states-general, and son to Elizabeth, Countess de Home, and Lewis de Nassau, Lord of Lecq, Beverwaert, and Odyk, natural son of Maurice, Prince of Orange, by Mademoiselle de Malines.

The French were masters of the Scheld and the canal of Bruges, and had not only broken down the banks near that town, but had cut several dikes to drown the country from the Scheld, and were strongly intrenched on that river to prevent the passage of the allies, and to favour the siege of Brussels, which the Duke of Bavaria undertook the 23rd of November, with a body of about sixteen or seventeen thousand men drawn from the garrison towns on the Scheld and the Maes.

The garrison consisted of five thousand men, under the command of Monsieur de Pascal, who, being summoned, refused to surrender, made the necessary dispositions for a vigorous defence, and by a letter acquainted the Duke of Marlborough with the danger he was in. His grace, on the 14th, at the head of a hundred squadrons and fifty battalions, and Prince Eugene with nineteen battalions and fifty squadrons, marched to the Scheld to force a passage spite of the enemy's intrenchments. This march was so secret that the French had not notice of the allies directing towards the Scheld, though they had received advice of their crossing the Lis. The Count de Lottum, on the 17th, about four in the morning, arrived with the vanguard near to Harlebeck River, and instantly laid two bridges, led over his troops, and drew up in order of battle.

The Duke of Marlborough, who had found means to pass the river at Kirkhoven, attacked the enemy so briskly at Berchem, that two hundred were slain, six hundred made prisoners, and the rest, with Monsieur Souternon, their commander, put to flight. The other French troops, posted near Oudenard, under the command of monsieur Hautefort, soon followed the example of their companions. Thus were rendered fruitless these intrenchments, which had cost the French so much care and fatigue; and the allies, beside a great quantity of stores, provisions, and baggage, with two standards and a pair of kettle-drums, which fell into their hands, had a free passage to march to the relief of Brussels; to which I must now return.

The trenches were opened before it on the 13th; on the 15th the Duke of Bavaria began to batter the town with great fury, between the gates of Namur and Louvain: at ten o'clock at night five or six thousand men attacked the covered way. The regiment of Dodignies, and the hussars, who defended it, resolutely stood the assault, which was repeated no less than nine times, and the fight having lasted till six in the morning, they left the covered way, and in their turn, falling in with the besiegers, retook all the posts they had lost, and made a prodigious slaughter of the enemy, whom they drove almost to their trenches.

It was reported as a certainty, that the besiegers lost in this action two thousand five hundred men, and the besieged eight hundred. The next day the elector did nothing further than batter the town; but all the spies agreed in their account of his being resolved to give a general assault the night following, and to cannonade the town with red balls, to make an insurrection of the *burghers*. Necessary dispositions were immediately made to repel the enemy, and to prevent the threatened conflagration. About eleven at night, when everyone expected the signal for the assault, news was brought that the whole camp of the enemy was in motion; and soon after that, they having had advice of the passing the Scheld by the allies, decamped with such precipitation that they left behind them their wounded, to the number of eight hundred men, sixteen pieces of cannon, four mortars, and a great deal of baggage, to retreat to Namur.

After the pass of the Rhine, and the raising the siege of Brussels, the allies divided their forces into several corps, that they might more easily subsist, secure a passage over the river, and cut off all the succours that the enemy might endeavour to throw into the citadel of Lisle; against which the trenches were opened on the 18th of October, and as the besiegers wanted powder, the works were carried on by sapping. As soon as they had made themselves masters of the glacis of the first counterscarp, they there fixed their batteries, and mounted their cannon on the third of November, at night.

After having taken several posts, they at last carried the second counterscarp, and mounted on it four pieces of battering cannon to play on the small work near the half-moon: thus far they had proceeded when Prince Eugene arrived. He commanded the sap to be continued, without firing a single gun to make a breach; for which reason, when everything was in readiness, on the 8th of December, the governor beat the chamade.

The capitulation being signed the next day, Prince Eugene and the Prince of Orange, *stadtholder*, or *stadhouder* of Frise, made a visit to marshal Boufflers's in the citadel, where they were received with a salute from the French cannon, and the marshal kept them company, when they returned. Next day the garrison marched out, following their baggage; the marshal, who was in the rear, conversed near half an hour with the Prince of Frise: all the officers saluted him with their half-pikes, which salutes he returned with his hat.

The Duke of Marlborough, after the siege of Brussels was raised, encamped at Alost. While we were here, I observed an officer, who, by his laced clothes, I conjectured to be one of the guards, strolling backwards and forwards in the intervals of the camp; I fancied he had a mind to steal some of our horses, and for that reason watched him narrowly; at length I saw him lead off a mare, belonging to a poor woman, into a ditch, and with her commit, by means of the bank, the most detestable sin that can enter into the thoughts of man. Colonel Irwin and another officer, both of Ingoldsby's regiment, happening at that instant to pass by, caught him in the fact, seized and gave him into the custody of the provost, where he remained till the duke, who had left the army, returned, when he was tried, condemned to the gallows, and executed accordingly.

As some of my readers may not know the provost's office, it will not be amiss to tell them that he attends the camp, and all offenders are put under his care, for which reason he commands a strong guard which goes everywhere with him; and the camp colour-men, who always precede the army, escorted by the forlorn hope, choose the strongest house they can meet with for his quarters, that he may secure his prisoners. When we march, the less criminals are handcuffed in the middle of a guard; but notorious ones are chained hand and foot, and put into the bread-waggons. The mare which this officer was enamoured with, was shot; but the duke first paid the poor woman who owned her, the full value.

Notwithstanding our army was extremely fatigued with the number of motions; that the fruits of our campaign were sufficient to cover our generals with glory; that winter was already begun, and the frosts very sharp, we, who imagined it would be carried no further, found ourselves deceived; for the duke could not think of leaving Ghent and Bruges in the possession of the French. To form the siege of the former, the Grand Army, under the command of the Duke of Marlborough, decamped from Bellem on the last of November, and marched in two columns to Marlebeck and Malle, situated on the lower Scheld; on the other hand, Prince Eugene, having five days after passed this river, encamped at Ename, and the town was the next day invested by Count de Lottum, the hereditary prince of Hesse-Cassel, and count de Tilly.

The Duke of Marlborough took up his quarters at Marlebeck, that he might be nearer to three attacks, one of which was on the side of the citadel, another between the imperial gate and that of

Brussels, and the third, between the gates of St. Peter and Courtray. While everything was preparing for opening the trenches, which was done on the 13th, and on the 14th, a detachment was sent to attack the Red-house on the canal of Sas van Ghent, where, as it is a place of importance, the French had left a garrison of two hundred men. These forces immediately raised their batteries, and made so furious a fire on the 15th, that the garrison, having in vain offered to surrender, on condition they might go off, were compelled to yield themselves prisoners of war.

In the meanwhile the allies pushed on their works before Ghent, had already got as far as the glacis of the counterscarp, and on the 18th, had a number of batteries of bombs and great guns ready, sufficient to reduce the town to a heap of rubbish; but the garrison not thinking it proper to expose the town to such ruin, sent the Prince of Isenghien, and two other captains, to the Duke of Marlborough, who allowed them to go out with all the marks of honour. Till the capitulation was got ready to sign, hostages were exchanged, and two gates of the town delivered up to us.

As the garrison had flattered themselves with being succoured, it was stipulated in the capitulation, that it should be void, if in a limited time, the French should draw near with an army and compel us to raise the siege. In effect, when the court of France had intelligence that Ghent was besieged, Marshal Boufflers with several general officers set out from Paris for Douay: but having advice by the way, that the town had capitulated, he turned back.

My husband in the siege was one of the forlorn hope, a body of men under the command of a lieutenant, ordered to lay the ropes and to direct the cutting of the trenches: we seldom expect to see any of these return again; but here the danger was greater than customary, as the night was clear, and they were soon descried by the sentinels; but so remarkably expeditious were our men, that they were all covered before the enemy had got their forces together to oppose them. As I always accompanied my husband, however dangerous it was, I, as usual, followed him this time, but Colonel Hamilton stopping me, and saying. 'Dear Kit, don't be so forward,'

I lost sight of him, and was some time hunting about before I could find him; for the ropes being lain, he with his companions were retired into a turnip field, and lay flat on their bellies, expecting the trench, which the workmen were throwing up, to cover them. Major Irwin told me where he was; and both the major and Lieutenant Stretton begged hard of me for some beer; but as I had but three flasks, and feared my husband might want, I had no pity for anyone else: as the night was very cold, and the ground wet, I had also provided myself with a bottle of brandy, and another of gin, for my dear Richard's refreshment. When I left these officers, I met a lieutenant known by the nickname of A—— and Pockets; a spent musket-ball had grazed on, and scratched his forehead, which his fright magnified to a cannon-ball. He desired I would show him to a surgeon; but his panic was so great, that I believe, had he been examined at both ends, he stood more in need of having his breeches shifted than his wound dressed.

In his fright he left his hat and wig, but they being found and restored him, and he at length assured his wound was no way dangerous, recovered his small share of spirits, but never his reputation; for he was called by everyone poltroon, and soon after broke as a coward. Leaving this Cotswold lion, I went to the turnip field, where I found my husband in the front rank, to whom my liquors were very comfortable. We stayed here till the trench was ready for us.

The next morning, as I was standing by Colonel Gossedge, he received a shot through the body; I gave him some beer and a dram, and carried him, though it was very dangerous, to Colonel Folke's quarters, for which piece of service the gentleman was extremely thankful, and promised, if he recovered, to reward me handsomely; but he died in three days. On my leaving him, I was sent for by the Duke of Argyle, to inform him what men we had lost. The next day, a drum of our regiment went into a very dangerous place to ease nature; I cautioned him against it, as I had observed the enemy pointed at or near that place: he did not heed my advice; but when he was buttoning up his breeches, a cannon-ball took off both his arms. The place where he rashly exposed himself, was so very dangerous, that not a man would venture to go to his assistance. I ran, therefore, and carried him off to a surgeon, under whose care he was in a fair way of doing well, but a cold he got killed him.

At a mile's distance from the town, out of danger, as I thought, of any shot from thence, and near the camp, I pitched my tent, which I stored from a garden belonging to a deserted brewhouse, that I had taken possession of. I had filled my tent with so many potatoes, carrots, turnips, &c. that I left but just room enough to sit down close by the door. One day a drake-shot from the enemy came in there, went through my tent into my garden, where I had turned my mare and an officer's horse, and killed the latter; I was luckily then a foraging, or I had infallibly been killed, as I always sat directly fronting my tent door. This obliged me to remove my tent further off, that I might be out of danger. While the siege continued, we had, one day, so severe and incessant rain, that not a man in the army had a dry thread on his back, which was followed by so severe a frost in the night, that a fire I had made before my tent, to dry myself and husband, I really believe, saved the lives of a number of our men. I burnt no less than forty faggots that night, which Colonel Godfrey gave me leave to take from a stack in his quarters. Two of our sentinels were found frozen to death.

When the two gates were given up, as I have already said, I got leave to go the day following into the town, where I made fifty shillings of the roots I carried in from the garden; for the garrison having secured to themselves what was in the town, and our men destroyed what was in the country, the scarcity made the *burghers* ready to give me my own price. The garrison went out of the town on the 22nd of December, fourteen thousand in number, with drums beating, colours flying, carrying with them six pieces of cannon, and were conducted by the way of Gaveren to Tournay. The next day the Duke of Marlborough entered the town, and was complimented at the gate by the magistracy, who presented him the keys in a gold basin.

The *burghers*, who had received the French with open arms, changed sides with their fortune, and made public rejoicings and thanksgivings in the churches for their departure, as a deliverance ardently wished for. These rejoicings were redoubled, on the news which soon after was brought, that the French had abandoned Bruges, and all the neighbouring posts. When the garrison of this town heard that Ghent, which was well fortified, had capitulated, finding themselves summoned by a trumpet in the Duke of Marlborough's name, they prepared for their retreat in earnest, fearing a longer delay might render it impossible: wherefore, on the 22nd of October, at night, they left the town, and withdrew on the side of Dixmude and Nieuport. At the same time the French abandoned Fort Plassendal, the village of Leffinghen, where they were intrenched, and all the posts they had in those quarters.

No sooner had the enemy quitted Bruges, but the magistrates sent deputies to the Duke of Marlborough to make their submission to King Charles. His grace received their submission, and garrisoned the town with two thousand men. Thus ended this glorious campaign; the army was ordered into winter-quarters; our regiment stayed in Ghent, where I got a comfortable living by cooking for, and selling beer to the soldiers. My horse cost me nothing this winter, having procured a sufficient stock of provision and straw at my first entrance into the town.

My husband having, by my interest, obtained leave to go out of town, which no garrison soldier can do under pain of death, without permission, we went out of the gate called the Sas, from the adjacent river of that name, to take a view of the country, and met a poor woman, who wept bitterly; I asked the reason of her tears, and she told me that she had three small children at home, and no way of providing for them, but by running *geneva* into the town; that the excise officers had lately seized a parcel, which had almost ruined her, and that now being on the point of venturing all she had, her late loss, and the fear she was in of being entirely undone, made her burst into a fit of crying.

In the Low Countries no duty is paid for what is not brought into a fortified town, but at the bringing anything within the gates it must pay a duty to the officers, stationed there to receive it, and to prevent defrauding the customs. We endeavoured to comfort the poor creature, and told her if she would step into the public house, which was near us, we would do our best to help her in running the *geneva* into the town. She very thankfully went in with us; she had eleven bladders, each would hold a stoop, ten of them were filled with *geneva*, and the eleventh with nastiness, which the country people keep in pits as the best manure for flax. I then thus divided the bladders; three I gave to my husband, two to the woman, the other five, and that designed for the officers, I took into my custody: three of the *geneva* bladders were tied round my waist next my skin, two round my neck, so that they fell under each arm, and were covered with my cloak, and the cleanly one I carried in my left hand, and though visibly, I pretended to endeavour to conceal it.

I went on in the direct road, but ordered them to go round a little lane, and when they saw the officers busy with me, to make a push for the town. I made for the gate; the officers, to my wish, perceived the bladder, and came up to me; I retreated, and keeping out of their reach, lured them away from, till I saw my comrades pretty near to, the gate; I then suffered them to come up to me, who demanded my *geneva*, laying hold of the bladder; I soon got it out of his hand who seized it, fell on my knees, and began a lamentable story of my poverty, large family, and sick children, for whose cure I had made a hard shift to purchase it. I amused them with this deplorable story till I saw my comrades within the barrier; but finding they were inexorable, and resolved to plunder me, I took my scissors, which hung by my side, and cutting the bladder, said. 'Since you must have it, e'en take it,' and flung the contents in his face.

One of his companions was coming up to seize me, but I showed him another bladder with my scissors, and he retreated, as 'tis probable he had an aversion to perfumes. I had now a free and open passage into the town, which I entered triumphant, with my bladder in my hand. I was no sooner in the town, but my husband and the woman met me; she was glad to see me safe, but when she found her liquors were so too, the poor creature wept for joy: and on relating my adventure, her laughter was as excessive, and had the same effect.

This success animated us to a second attempt. The excise-men saw me, and cried out. 'There's the retailer of soil;' I answered, They should find I dealt by wholesale, if ever they offered to disturb me. In short, we often passed with our cargoes, none daring to molest us; till a new officer, who did not know me, was set on by the others; but as I always went with a charge, he repented his temerity, for I gave him so fetid a reception, that I thought he would have brought his heart up. His brethren abused me at a distance, but did not care to come to a close engagement; their language, however, was so provoking, that I threatened for the future to carry a pistol, and blow their brains out, the first time they durst come within my reach.

I did indeed arm myself as I had threatened, but I had neither powder nor ball; however, as they had been told my history, I was so terrible to these poltroons, that I believe I might have kept them in awe with a black pudding. Beside the above, I fell upon another stratagem to deceive those harpies the officers of the customs. It was this; I had a large spaniel which I brought up from a puppy; he was of the water breed, and had such a rough coat, that every half year it fetched me three shillings from a hatter. This dog, who had been taught to fetch and carry, we used to go out with, furnished with oily cakes, to the town ditch, where we lay concealed, my husband and the dog on one side, I on the other in the weeds, till the smugglers came with horseloads of brandy, &c. and in small kegs; two or three of these we tied together with a rope, and giving the dog the end in his mouth, he would, on my husband's calling, swim over to him, and he rewarded him with a cake, after which he would return at my call, with the empty rope. This method was repeated till all was got over, which they carried into the town, and we retired till morning, when we entered the gate publicly. The smugglers paid us three crowns a night for our dog and attendance.

At this place I was with child, and longed for eels, which one Hugh Jones ventured his life, by going out of town without leave, to get for me, by robbing the wicker baskets in the moat: I mention this because he was afterwards my second husband, and often had attempted my virtue, in the life of my first, who for the tenderness he showed me in this action, bequeathed me to him in case of survivorship. Indeed he took all opportunities to gain my affections, and convince me of his own; and I must acknowledge it was to his assiduity and tenderness, that next to God, I owed the preservation of my life, when I was ill and not able to help myself; in which time he also took care of and supported my mare.

There was at this time a pretty young fellow in garrison with us, a volunteer, but in whose regiment I cannot readily call to mind; he was the younger son of a gentleman of good fortune, who gave him so handsome an allowance, that he maintained a servant and two horses; dressed as well as any officer, and kept the best company; he was very forward in every action; never shunned, but rather courted danger; and, in the midst of the greatest, always showed a great composure of mind in his countenance: he was not above eighteen, but very reserved, and somewhat haughty. This gentleman resented the freedom I took with some officers where he was in company, and told me I was very impertinent.

The affront nettled me so much, that I called him a *petit maitre*, and said, if it would not be a disgrace to me to set my wit to boys, I would teach him better manners, by giving him the correction his ill breeding called for. He answered with a *pish* only, and turning his back on me, said to a captain. 'You see the fruits of making mean people familiar: you ought indeed to bear with it, because you have encouraged her taking such liberties, and those brought her impertinence upon you; but 'tis hard upon me, who always have avoided her.'

'You will do well,' replied I, 'to be careful in avoiding me for the future;' and went home in a passion, dressed myself in one of my husband's suits, (for he had two very handsome ones I had bought him out of my capital, which was not yet quite exhausted,) put on my silver-hilted sword, and went to a young woman's house whom the cadet visited. I asked for her, and being introduced, desired to speak with her in private. As soon as she had carried me into a room, and seated herself, desiring me to sit, she asked my business.

'Madam,' said I, 'to be short with you, I have often seen, and as often admired you; I am now come to tell you the passion you have inspired, which I can no longer conceal; it gives me too great torture. I know you have some engagements with a young English cadet, which have hurt your reputation: but to give you the most convincing proof of my fondness, if you will promise to cast him off, and never see him more, I will not only marry you, but maintain you as the wife of an English gentleman of fortune, as I pretend, and you will find me to be, and promise on my honour, never to reproach you with your former life.'

'Sir,' said she, 'you are very free with my character.'

'Madam,' replied I, 'not more so than the world; for I learned it from common fame.'

'Which,' answered my damsel, 'you will allow a common liar: however, sir, you talk so much like a man of honour, that I can forgive the liberty you have taken, and desire a little time to consider on what you have proposed.'

I told her, what she might term but a small space, a man as passionately in love as I was, would count an age: 'I will give you to consider,' continued I, 'till tomorrow ten o'clock, which is not less, by my computation, than a month's delay'; and rising up, saluted her, and took my leave. I was punctual to my hour the next morning, and she told me, she accepted my conditions, and as a proof that she would be just to them, said, I last night refused to see the cadet, notwithstanding he was very urgent. I stayed with her three hours, in which time I had promised her mountains; a life which should be but one continued round of pleasure, and an affection which no time should have force to alter. During my visit, I had the satisfaction to hear her servant tell the cadet, who came to see his mistress, that she was not at home, and that she had left word, in case he came to the house, in her absence, that she should take it as a favour, his giving over visiting her, which would beside save him a fruitless trouble.

He said, 'I suppose she has some new favourite, I shall find him out;' and flung away in a rage, which gave me the most sensible pleasure. I took my leave soon after, and was going home to shift my dress, when I spied my cadet at a little distance, who watched his mistress's door. He hastened after me, and asked what business I had in that house which he saw me come out of.

'Sir,' said I, 'by what authority do you ask me?'

'Here,' said he, 'is my commission to examine you,' laying his hand on his sword; and I, doing the like, replied, 'Here is my reason for not answering you.'

We both drew, the moment my husband passed by, who, knowing me, also drew, and got between us, saying. 'My dear Kitty, what's the meaning of this?'

At these words, the cadet, looking earnestly in my face, knew me, put up his sword, laughed heartily, and taking me by the hand, said, 'Let us be friends for the future; I am glad I have not a more dangerous rival; come Kit, I'll give you and your husband a bottle and bird for dinner.'

'You see,' said I, 'what it is to affront me; for I have made but two visits to your mistress, and in them have made such a progress, that you have been twice refused entrance.'

An officer of our acquaintance coming by, he prevailed on him to keep us company. The cadet carried us to the Couronne Imperiale, where he ordered a handsome dinner; after which we drank a hearty bottle, were very merry with the manner of my revenge; he begged pardon for having affronted me, promised he would be no more guilty, and entreated me to undeceive his mistress, whom he could easily forgive agreeing to honourable and such alluring conditions as I had offered. I reconciled them, and we were all good friends the little time he stayed in the Low Countries, which was but ten days after; for his elder brother dying by a hurt he received by a fall in hunting, his father sent for him over, and he carried his lady with him to England.

I have already said that a very great frost immediately followed the taking of Ghent, and that two of our sentinels were found frozen to death. This frost continued, and was so terribly severe, that a number of people, fruit trees, and sown seed, perished by the cold. This hard winter occasioned a very great scarcity, and excessively raised the price of all manner of provisions, especially in France, where almost all the vines were frost-nipped to the very roots: so that of many years before, that kingdom had not been in so deplorable a situation. The treasury was exhausted by the expense of the war; trade was interrupted by the number of ships the two maritime powers kept constantly cruising in all parts of the seas to prevent the importation of goods; the farmer was not only incapable of paying his rent, but even of supplying the towns with necessary provisions; in a word, they were in the utmost desolation.

To the cries of the miserable harassed people were joined public acts of devotion to appease the anger of heaven, to deprecate their then present miseries, and to obtain a speedy peace, which they looked upon as the only remedy to these oppressive evils. The king gave his people to understand that he was sensibly touched with their sufferings, and declared that he was inclined to give them peace, whatever it cost him. In effect, he sent Messieurs Voisin and Rouille, to Holland, in appearance upon the affair of the fishery; but in earnest, to set on foot a negotiation with the allies. The secret was so closely kept all the time the conferences were held at the Hague, that no one had any certain knowledge of what was upon the carpet; but the number of extraordinary couriers, which were observed to pass and repass, gave some inkling of a treaty of peace, and hopes of a happy issue; more especially when they saw the Duke of Marlborough, who had been at all the conferences, go for England on the 2nd of May, and return again on the 15th, N.S., accompanied by Lord Townshend, whom the queen had honoured with the character of envoy extraordinary, to treat on a peace.

The French king sent Messieurs Torcy and Pajot, to hasten its conclusion. Notwithstanding the protest made by King Philip, that he would never renounce the crown of Spain, but was resolved, on the contrary, to maintain his right to it by the sword to the last drop of his blood, the conferences were carried on more briskly than ever, and sometimes protracted to midnight. On the 28th of May, N. S., articles were prepared and signed by the plenipotentiaries of the allies. Beside a great number of towns in the Low Countries, on the Rhine and elsewhere, which France gave up by these articles. Charles was declared in them lawful king of all the Spanish monarchy; and it was agreed that Philip and his family should quit that kingdom by the 1st of September, and in case of his refusal, that the king of France should join his arms to those of the allies, to compel him by force.

Messieurs Torcy and Pajot set out for the court of France with the preliminaries agreed upon; but at the time that everyone thought the peace in a manner concluded, advice came that Lewis XIV. could never consent to assist in dethroning his grandson, and for that reason had rejected the articles: thus vanished all the hopes conceived of the pacification of Europe.

The negotiations of peace had not suspended the necessary preparations for continuing the war; upon their being broken off, Mr. Rouille set out on his return to France on the 9th of June, N. S., and the Duke of Marlborough on the same day for the army.

The French being intrenched near Arras, in a camp covered with woods and marshes, which rendered it impracticable to approach them, the duke turned back upon Tournay, a very strong town, where Monsieur de Surville commanded a garrison of four thousand men. We invested the place on the 27th of June, N. S., and while preparations were making to open the trenches, the Prince of Orange, *stadtholder* of Frise, at the head of thirty squadrons and twelve battalions, appeared before, and made himself master of St. Amand, and at the same time another detachment took Fort de la Scarpe sword in hand.

In the interim, the line of circumvallation was finished, and several thousand fascines, gabions, palisades, and other materials necessary for the works, were got together, and the trench was opened on the 7th of July, N. S., before the castle, by four battalions and two thousand workmen under the command of Count Lottum; before the hornwork of the seven fountains, by three battalions and two thousand workmen, commanded by General Schulemburg; and by General Fagel, at the head of the like number of soldiers and pioneers near the gate of Marville. Notwithstanding the diligence of the besiegers, the siege was likely to prove a very tedious one, because the boats on which the artillery was embarked could not get up the Scheld higher than Oudenard on account of the shallowness of the water, and the banks raised by the French the preceding year to turn its course, several of which were yet standing.

However, this obstacle was obviated by cutting a new canal; and the artillery being at length arrived, we began on the 13th to batter the outworks. Assisted by the fire of our batteries, General Fagel pushed on his works to the very brink of the ditch, which on the 17th he began to fill up. Count Lottum was on the same day pretty near as far advanced with his; and the night before, Baron de Schulemburg having carried the hornworks sword in hand, made a lodgement there, and moreover possessed himself of a neighbouring ravelin. Monsieur de Surville finding himself thus straitened, on the 28th, between seven and eight in the evening, hung out the white flag at the three attacks. The capitulation was signed the next morning, and the garrison withdrew into the citadel, all the works of which were mined.

At the expiration of the truce agreed upon, to give garrison time to retire into the citadel, Count Lottum and the Baron de Schulemburg attacked it in two different places, and a re-enforcement of thirty battalions and six squadrons were sent them from the Grand Army. Four days after the opening the trench, Monsieur de Ravignan, sent by the French king, arrived in the camp of the besiegers, and having obtained leave to speak to one of the officers of the citadel, the governor sent the next day a project of agreement to the allies, by which he engaged to surrender on the 5th, of September, if he was not before succoured; all hostilities were to cease during that interval, between the besiegers and besieged, and a gate of the citadel was to be given up to the former on the 8th of August, if the king of France approved the agreement; for whose approbation monsieur de Ravignan returned to the court; but nothing was concluded upon, because the king insisted on extending the truce to the two armies; wherefore the fire was again begun, and surely never was so much fire seen from beneath the earth.

As the citadel was everywhere mined round, notwithstanding all the industry and fatigue of the allies to discover them, they played off no less than thirty-eight, at only Count Lottum's attack, in twenty-six days' time; so that we often saw hundreds of men at once fly into the air, and fall down again piecemeal, or buried alive; and if any were dug out living, they were miserably shattered in their limbs, or half roasted. Very often the miners on either side, met and fought with as much fury underground, as they did in the trenches: however, the place was so violently attacked, that the governor hung out the white ensign on the 31st of August N. S., but as the besiegers would allow him no other terms than his surrendering prisoner of war, he broke off the parley, and threatened he would blow all up before he would surrender on such terms.

On this the siege was once more begun, and the governor given to understand, that if he persisted in his design he must expect no quarter. This threat made him change his desperate resolution, and he accepted the conditions offered him; but with a promise that the garrison should be exchanged as soon as possible, for a like number of prisoners taken by the French.

My husband's regiment was one of those that attacked the citadel. One day Lord Cobham coming into the trench, ordered the engineer to point a gun at a windmill between us and the citadel, and promised a guinea to whoever fired and brought it down; I immediately snatched the match out of the man's hand who was going to fire, clapped it to the touchhole, and down came the windmill. Major Petit, before I fired, bid me take care the cannon did not recoil upon me, or break the drums of my ears, which I had forgot to stop. I was in too much haste to get the guinea, and not minding the caution, I was beat backwards, and had the noise of the cannon a long while after in my ears. The officers could not refrain laughing to see me set on my backside; but as I was not hurt, I had, according to the proverb. Let him laugh that wins, the most reason to be merry about the mouth, for Lord Cobham, always better than his word, gave me two guineas, saying, I was a bold wench, instead of one he promised me; general Fagel gave me another, and four officers gave me a *ducat* apiece.

Soon after, Captain Brown mounting the trench, had his leg so miserably shattered by a musket-shot, that the surgeon was obliged to cut it off. His servants and nurses not having the courage to hold the candle, I performed that office, and was very intent on the operation, which no way shocked me, as it was absolutely necessary.

During this siege, or indeed any other, I never lost an opportunity of marauding; to this end I was furnished with a grappling iron and a sword, for I must acquaint my reader, that, on the approach of an army, the boors throw their plate, copper, &c., into wells; their linen they bury in chests, and for their own security they get into fortified towns, or under the shelter of some strong place. With my grapple I searched all the wells I met with, and got good booty, sometimes kitchen utensils, brass pails, pewter dishes, &c.; sometimes a silver spoon. With my sword, which I carried to discover what was buried, I bored the ground, where I found it had been lately stirred. This I learned of the Dutch soldiers in Ireland when King William was there; for they discovered by this method, and took away a chest of linen my mother had hid under ground, with a large quantity of wheat.

While I was one day busied in search of plunder, I heard behind me a great burst, like a sudden short clap of thunder, and turning nimbly round, I saw the air full of shattered limbs of men. This happened, as I was informed at my return, by a spark from a pipe of tobacco setting fire to a bomb, by which fifty shells and twenty-four of our men were blown up; but luckily, our magazine of powder, though near the same place, escaped. As I have often said, wherever my husband was ordered upon duty, I always followed him, and he was sometimes of the party. that went to search for and draw the enemy's mines; I was often engaged with their party underground, where our engagements were more terrible than in the field, being sometimes near suffocated with the smoke of straw which the French fired to drive us out; and the fighting with pickaxes and spades, in my opinion, was more dangerous than with swords.

I have, in the journal of the siege, taken notice of the number of mines sprung; one of which blew up four hundred of our men, and another narrowly missed carrying up a whole regiment, which was just drawn off as it was fired, so that the designed execution was by accident prevented, and only eight men lost.

After having hastily filled up the works before Tournay, the Prince of Hesse-Cassel began his march at the head of sixteen thousand, men, to invest Mons, the capital of Hainault, and to take possession of some posts in its neighbourhood, especially along the River Trouille, which runs by that town. On the 4th of September he was followed by the rest of the army, but the rains and the straitness of the ways was such an hindrance to our march, that the French had time enough, having also decamped, to march to Blangies, and post their horse in a plain between two woods, in which they had placed their infantry. The allies, at their arrival, found the enemy thus posted, and resolved to attack and drive them from their camp: but as they would undertake nothing, without the assent of the deputies of the States, who were not yet come up; the French took the advantage of that time to make their camp inaccessible, by covering it with a triple intrenchment.

Notwithstanding this new obstacle, the allies prepared for a battle, early in the morning, on the 11th, N. S.; and with all imaginable resolution, at eight o'clock, marched up to the intrenchments. Our left wing, commanded by the duke, charged with such bravery, that we drove the French out of the two first intrenchments, cutting all to pieces that opposed us; but could not force the third, which was defended by a great many pieces of cannon, and felled trees laid athwart: however, we some time maintained the ground we had got upon the enemy, though exposed to the fire of their artillery, which swept down whole companies at a time; but at length, seeing our number terribly diminished, we were obliged to abandon the two intrenchments we had carried.

In the meanwhile the foot of the right, commanded by Prince Eugene, having made through the wood into the plains, after a most obstinate resistance of the French, gave the horse an opportunity also to force the intrenchment joining to the wood. The horse on both sides were engaged with an unparalleled fury: but the allies continually getting ground, as their troops entered the intrenchments, the advantage was visibly on their side: they put to flight the main battle, and by that gave an opportunity to their left wing, which had returned to the attack, to recover the two intrenchments, which they could not before keep, and also to carry the third: this was followed by an entire defeat of the French army; which, at three in the afternoon, took to flight, and in its turn, by the confusion they fled in, lost a great number of men, so that the slaughter on both sides was really terrible; for, as far as I could see, the ground was covered with dead and dying men. The allies lost fourteen thousand men killed, wounded, or prisoners: the French nineteen thousand.

The night before the Battle of Taisnieres, Lieutenant-General De-dem went off with a detachment to throw himself into St. Guilain, which the Duke of Marlborough was assured, the French garrison had abandoned; but the general, in his march, receiving certain advice to the contrary, instead of two hundred foot, which he designed to send thither from Genap, drew from thence five hundred, and sustained them with two squadrons. Colonel Haxhuisen, who commanded this detachment, sent a drum to summon the garrison, having, as he drew near the town, extended his front, that he might make a greater show of number: on a refusal to surrender, he gave the assault that very day; and after a quarter of an hour's dispute he carried a barricade, and advanced behind a house on the right of the battery; on which the chamade was beat; but as they had not done it soon enough, they were forced to surrender prisoners of war.

Our army now invested Mons, into which the French found means, eight days after the battle, to introduce a convoy of ammunitions, provisions, money, and a thousand men; the trenches were opened on the 25th over against Fort Berteaumont, by the engineer General Hartel, with four battalions, and two thousand workmen; and before the gate of Havre by two battalions, and also two thousand workmen under the command of the engineer De Bauffe. We were terribly hindered by the rains, which obliged us to bottom the trenches with fascines, and to drain them by cutting a long gut, which reached as far as the Trouille: but notwithstanding all obstacles, we pushed on our approaches so briskly, that having finished our batteries, we were ready to give the assault to the hornwork near Berteaumont gate, on the 20th of October: the garrison, however, prevented us, by beating the chamade.

Deputies came out of the town, and returned again by eight o'clock with the articles of capitulation, which they brought back the next morning with the governor's approbation. At eleven o'clock we were put into possession of Nimy gate; two days after the garrison marched out; the French were conducted to Maubeuge, the Spaniards and Bavarians to Namur. The reduction of this town terminated the campaign in Flanders.

When we left Tournay, and before the investing of Mons, as the army marched towards the French lines, I chose to go with the camp colour-men, who, attended by the forlorn hope, march at so considerable a distance before the army, that they are often cut off before any force can come up to their assistance; which, though it makes it the most dangerous post, it is the most profitable, if there is any plunder to be got, as there are but few to share it. In our march, I espied at some distance a great house, which I, advancing before the camp colourmen, ran to, leaving my horse to the care of a sick sergeant, who was glad of the opportunity to ride.

I here found six couple of fowls with their legs tied, a basket of pigeons, and four sheep, which were also tied and ready to be carried off; but I suppose, upon our appearance, the people made the best of their way to secure things of greater value. One of the sheep I killed, dressed, cut off a leg, and all the fat. The other three I loosed, and turned into the yard; by the time I had done, our men came up with me, and I put the carcass of the sheep on my mare before the sergeant; the fowls I hung about my neck; drove my sheep before me, and so marched to the place designed for the camp, called Havre. Being here arrived, while they were fixing boughs for the disposition of the camp, and marking out ground for every regiment, I pitched my tent near a deserted public house, allotted for colonel Hamilton's quarters; turned my sheep to grass, and hung up my mutton on a tree to cool: I then went into the colonel's quarters, over which, as soon as it was appointed, a guard was set; but by a bribe, I struck him so blind, that he could not see me and my husband's comrades, who lent a friendly hand, carry off a large quantity of faggots, hay and straw for my mare and my own bed; fill all my empty flasks with beer, and roll off a whole barrel to my tent.

Having made these prizes, I cut up my mutton, laid by a shoulder to roast, the neck and breast to make broth; dug a hole with a hatchet to boil my pot in, which, the fire being made, I set on with the mutton and sweet herbs, and was enjoying myself by a glorious fire, when the army came up. Colonel Hamilton and Major Erwood came to my fire, and were not a little surprised to see I had gotten so many things in readiness. I showed them my provisions of all sorts; upon which the colonel, suspecting that I had plundered his quarters, asked where I had got my barrel of strong beer. I told him, that falling in with some boors, I drove them before me, and made them bring me what I wanted; to which he civilly replied, 'D—n you, you are a lying devil.'

'Come,' said I, 'you mutton-monger, will you give me *handsel?*' They called for a gallon of beer, and drinking a little, gave the rest among some of the men, and ordered the shoulder of mutton to be roasted, which I did by pitching two forked sticks into the ground, putting it on a jointed spit, and setting a soldier's wife to turn it. I made four crowns apiece of my sheep, besides the fat, which I sold to a woman who made mould candles for the men, and made a good penny of my fowls and pigeons. A body of troopers and some hussars, being ordered out to reconnoitre in the woods at Taisnieres, before the enemy intrenched themselves, and to cover the foragers, with strict charge to return at the firing of a cannon, I, being one of the foragers, took my mare along with me, leaving another horse which I had bought of a hussar in an orchard, near Brigadier Lalo's quarters, and digging a hole, I buried my money.

When we were some distance from the camp, I pushed forward, on which Quarter-Master Hankey and Lieutenant Mackenny bid me not be too venturesome; I answered, that I saw no danger, and hastened on to a large house, which I entered, and found a bed readymade, two or three tubs of flower; an oven full of hot bread, a considerable quantity of bacon and beef hanging in the chimney, a basket full of cocks and hens, with two pots of butter. I emptied the feathers out of the tick to cover my mare with, lest the hot bread should burn her back, then threw the feathers out of the bolster, into one end of which I put my bread, and into the other my beef and bacon; my pots of butter I slung on each side of her, took my fowls in my hand, and mounted; which I had scarcely done when I heard the signal gun, an alarm given the foragers, that the whole body of the enemy was coming upon us; and that their seeming to march to the left, was only to cover the filing off their infantry into the woods.

The terror with which the foragers were struck at the news is hardly credible; the fields were strewed with corn, hay, and utensils, which they had not the courage to take along with them; nay some, whose horses were at a little distance, rather chose to lose, than venture to fetch them: I jogged on towards the army, but seeing a fine truss of hay lying, and fearing my horses might want, the danger could not make me withstand the temptation; I leaped off my mare, clapped it upon her, and mounting again, got safe to the place where the army lay. I was surprised to see all in motion; however, I stayed to kill my fowls, fetch my horse, and money that I had buried, strike my tent, with which, and other things, I loaded him, and followed the army.

My husband being in the rear, I had an opportunity of conversing with him; he was extremely melancholy, and told me this engagement would most certainly be the last he should ever see: I endeavoured to laugh him out of this notion, but he insisted upon it that he should be killed, which proved but too true. In our march, so heavy a rain fell, that we were ankle deep, and seeing a little child of one of my husband's comrades, I took it up lest it should be lost in the deep clay. At night, when in sight of the enemy, our army halted, and lay that night on some fallow ground, on which were many heaps of dung, and he was a happy man who could get one to sleep upon. I left the army, and went to a great house in the rear to dress my provisions; I led my horses into the house, which by the help of one Armstrong, a butcher, and of Lord Orkney's French baker, I unloaded.

Next I made a great wood fire, with what I found, dried myself and the child, and laid it on some straw before the fire. I had now leisure to look out for forage for my beasts, and found some flax, hay, and clover; with the first I littered them, threw the other before them, and looking them up in a handsome parlour, thought of dressing some victuals; in order to which I went to the well for water, and found a bucket, which is not common, for the boors, as they had several things in the wells, commonly cut them away. In letting down my bucket I thought it struck against something which sounded like a brass kettle; I was not out; for, letting down my drag, I brought one up; and at the next throw I fetched out a brass pail, in which was a silver quart mug in a fish-skin case.

I made several other casts, but brought up nothing more: wherefore, leaving the well, having taken what water I wanted, I set it on the fire, pulled my fowls, which, with some of my hung beef and bacon, I clapped into the pot, and then stepped into the garden to cut some sprouts, washed and put them in, and leaving the care of the cooking to Armstrong and the baker, strolled over the house for plunder; but after searching several rooms, I found nothing worth carrying off, but what was too cumbersome; wherefore I visited the cellar, where I found, to my great joy, a barrel of excellent strong beer. I immediately ran up for, and filled my pails; as I was returning with these full, I happened to stumble against an inward cellar-door, which, flying open, discovered another small one: I hastened up with my beer, full of hopes of finding somewhat better worth within the little door. I found two rundlets and two quart bottles of vinegar, and two more of very good brandy, with which I filled my flasks, and placed all my booty in the parlour, where my beasts were shut up.

My provisions being ready, I clapped them and a quantity of beer on one of my mares, having first regaled my two assistants; who were not a little thankful, for provision was then so scarce in the army, a guinea and half was offered for an ounce of bread, and there was no probability of getting any supply till the battle was over, which we expected would be, and, as I have already shown, was, very bloody. I filled the child's belly, filled her apron with victuals, and taking her with me, left her with her father, whom I soon found, and who was very ill of an ague, lying in a miserable condition on a heap of dung. He would fain have had me take care of her, but I could not undertake the charge. Leaving her, I went in search of my husband; and after a considerable time, as there was so great a fog I could scarce see a yard before me, I met with one of our regiment, who cried out. 'Here comes the picture of plenty.'

I asked for my husband, and he showed him fast asleep, with his head on his comrade's backside. I awakened him, and bid him ask what officers or soldiers he thought fit to eat with him, especially such as he was obliged to; for I had brought a large quantity of provisions. I set the bread, butter, and beef, before his comrades, who, sitting down on the dung, made a hearty meal, though they had no tablecloth, knives, &c.; reserving the bacon, fowls, and sprouts, for my husband and the invited officers, who were Colonel and Captain Hamilton, Colonel Irwin, Captain Ross, Major Maclane, and Colonel Folks. Two fowls, some bacon and beef, I gave to my husband and his sergeant; when every one of these were satisfied, I gave the remainder of my provisions to some young recruits, who, not being inured to hardships, were ready to perish with hunger.

I had set apart some pullets with eggs for the general officers, and sought out my Lord Orkney, whom I found with the Generals, Lumley, Webb, Withers, and Lord North and Grey. As soon as Lord Orkney saw me, he asked if I had any beer to give him. I answered, I had enough, at his lordship's service, but I thought he had better eat before he drank.

'That's true,' said my lord, 'if I knew where to get it, but I don't believe there is anything in the army.'

'You guess pretty near the truth,' I replied, 'for I don't believe any one has a morsel except myself, and if you could take up with fowl, bacon, sprouts, and hung beef, I have them ready at your service;' and set them before him. This was a very agreeable surprise to them all;

they tore the meat with their fingers, and eat very heartily; but wanting water to mix with their wine, on some soldier's refusal, I went to the well within musket-shot of the enemy, and fetched them some. I remember one of the company proposed a motion of the army, not only without the Duke of Marlborough's order, but contrary to his express command, which was to keep ourselves in readiness to march on the word given. Lord Orkney said, they ought to wait till his grace's orders came, for he durst say he knew better than any in the company when to give them, and thought it was their duty to wait.

On this, another, whose name I purposely conceal, said, that his grace was gone into the wood in close conference with his nephew the duke of Berwick, and wished it was not to sell the army of the allies: Lord Orkney, with some warmth, answered, that it was ungenerous as unjust to harbour a thought so injurious to the duke's honour, and so contrary to his nature that he would be bound body for body, that he was incapable of anything which could cast a blemish on his exalted character, than which no man breathing could, with justice, boast a greater, nay, he knew none that could equal him. The Duke of Argyle joined the company, and soon after, went open-breasted among the men to encourage them to behave as became Englishmen; 'you see, brothers,' said he, 'I have no concealed armour, I am equally exposed with you, and I require none to go where I shall refuse to venture: remember you fight for the liberties of all Europe, and the glory of your nation, which shall never suffer by my behaviour; and I hope the character of a Briton is as dear to every one of you.'

To do him justice, he always fought were the danger was greatest, and encouraged the soldiers more by his actions than by his words. The Duke of Marlborough had indeed a conference with the Duke of Berwick, which gave him an opportunity to view the enemy's batteries, which was of signal service to us. At his return, he gave orders for the cutting fascines, which were to fill up a morass between us and the French; after which, a battery was raised, and our guns playing upon the French battery soon dismounted the cannon which the duke had noted, and was covered by the wood, by which the intrenchment was more accessible. I have already given an account of this battle, wherefore I shall only observe, that the English guards first entered the wood, and, though they behaved gallantly, were repulsed with prodigious loss; our regiment seconded their attack, and was as roughly handled.

I entered the wood with small beer for my husband; though the shot and bark of trees flew thicker than my reader, if he has not seen action, can well imagine; not a few pieces of the latter fell on my neck, and gave me no small uneasiness by getting down my stays. My dog, which I have before mentioned, at the entrance of the wood, howled in a pitiful manner, which surprised me, as it was unusual.

A man near me, who was easing nature, said. 'Poor creature, he would fain tell you that his master is dead'.

'How,' said I, 'is he dead!'

'I know not,' replied he, 'if he is dead or not, but I am sure he is very much wounded.' This brought into my mind his foreboding that he should be killed in this battle. I was almost out of my wits; but though I feared the worst, my hopes of finding him alive supported me. I ran among the dead, and turned over near two hundred, among whom I found Brigadier Lalo, Sir Thomas Pendergrass, and a great number more of my best friends, before I found my husband's body, which a man, who was a stranger to me, though I was not unknown to him, was stripping. At my approach he went off, and left his booty, fearing the effects of the rage I was in at the sight of my dead husband; and I certainly had killed him, could I have laid my hands on him; for I was in so great a fury, that I bit out a great piece out of my right arm, tore my hair, threw myself on his corpse, and should have put a period to my life had I had any instrument of death.

Here I lay some time before my tears flowed, which at length gushed forth in such abundance, that I believe the stream saved my life, at least my senses. While I was deploring my loss, Captain Ross came by, who, seeing my agony, could not forbear sympathising with me, and dropped some tears, protesting that the poor woman's grief touched him nearer than the loss of so many brave men. This compassion from the captain gave me the nickname of Mother Ross; by which I became better known than by that of my husband. After my tears had a little relieved me, I took my husband's body, laid it across my mare, which I led into the ground, dug a grave, buried him, and would have thrown myself into the same pit, had not some of his comrades, who were at hand, prevented me.

Seeing I was prevented, I mounted my mare, though almost naked, for I had in my distraction torn off great part of my clothes, and pushed. into the wood, notwithstanding I had no arms, to wreak my vengeance on the French, of whom our army was then in pursuit, resolving to tear in pieces whoever fell into my hands: nay, had I had strength and opportunity, I would have given no quarter to any man in the French army. I was running full speed after them, and was near Mambeuge when Captain Usher laid hold of my mare and forced me back, or I had infallibly been either killed or taken.

The former I did not think a misfortune; but mine did not end with my pursuit, for my distraction rendered me incapable of looking after my business, giving myself up to my grief and tears, which employed my whole time for seven days, in transports running to my husband's grave and endeavouring to remove the earth with my hands, that I might have another view of the dear man, whom I loved with greater tenderness than I did myself, and for whose safety I would not have hesitated at sacrificing my own life. I always found my poor dog lying on his master's grave; but at my drawing near, he ran to the rear of the regiment, where my poor husband used to be while living. The poor creature's gratitude was so great, that for eight days I could not get him to eat anything: our removal from the place, and time, mitigated his visible grief. I myself, though often importuned, touched nothing of sustenance for a whole week. The Prince of Orange, near whose quarters my tent was pitched, and who heard my cries, was so charitable as to order his servants to fetch me to meals, saying, 'The poor woman weeps night and day, and will, I fear, kill herself, which would grieve me'

They obeyed his highnesses compassionate orders, and would set the choicest meats before me, but I could touch nothing; I only enjoyed the comfort of the fire, and the liberty of taking coals to make me one in my tent. The first who prevailed on me to touch meat, was a Scotch Cameronian, who forced me to a tent where he had got a breast of mutton; but I was so weak that I could not support the smell of the meat, but fainted away with the first bit between my teeth; lay a long time as dead, and was brought to my senses by very slow degrees; which Colonel Hamilton's lady hearing, she sent for me, and ordered what was more suitable to my condition.

After I had eat a little, she endeavoured to divert my melancholy, and frequently would have me to dinner with her, at which time she would chide me in a gay manner for grieving for one man so much, when the battalion afforded a number, out of which I might pick and choose; sometimes, again, she would very gravely represent to me the sin of self-murder, which would be the consequence of indulging to my grief. That it was, beside, disputing the will of God, which we ought to obey with resignation, and not presumptuously to call his will in question. Colonel Hamilton often seconded his lady's charity, and in about six weeks I began to get the better of my grief, though it was long before I could entirely shake it off. In this time my affairs went backward; I had neglected everything, and left my tent to the care of a drummer and his wife, who were so good as to consume my whole substance by sinking the produce of my effects, and their generosity to such as came to sponge under the pretence of visits of condolence.

My mares fared better than I did; for one Hugh Jones, a grenadier, whom I have before mentioned, took them under his care, and provided them every night with forage, which he got from Captain Hume's stables. He had often solicited me in my husband's time, but finding me entirely averse to even the thoughts of injuring my husband, he gave over his suit, and esteemed me for my honesty. My husband being dead, this esteem was changed to love; he now renewed his suit, and courted me for a wife. His care of my mares, his having ventured his life to save my longing when I was with child at Ghent, and his daily endeavouring to oblige me, together with his threats of putting an end to his life if I continued obstinate, prevailed on me to marry him in the camp, about eleven weeks after my husband's decease, on condition that he should not eat or bed with me till we were in garrison, which he agreed to, and kept his promise, however contrary to his inclinations.

My marriage being known, had like to have caused a duel between a sergeant and my new husband, the former saying, *The cow that lows most after her calf went soonest to bull;* the latter took him up in a very sharp manner, and if others had not interposed, and made them friends, after the sergeant had acknowledged that he was in the wrong to reflect upon me, he might have repented his being witty.

After the reduction of Mons, our regiment was garrisoned at Ghent, where we spent the winter without any event worthy of notice; wherefore I shall pass over this winter season, and go on to the operations of the ensuing campaign, after I have taken a short view of affairs in Spain; as this year was fought the Battle of Almenara, where we quitted scores with the Spaniards for the loss we sustained in that of Almanza. The emperor sent his brother King Charles some troops from Italy, which arrived very opportunely to check the progress of the enemy, who had carried the town and castle of Alicant; defeated the Portuguese in the plain of Guadiana, and lived at discretion in their country. Philip himself took the field, and directed his march to Catalonia; but having intelligence that the French were ordered to run no hazard, he returned to Madrid very much dissatisfied, and there found a general consternation on the intelligence they had of the king of France having recalled his troops.

Resolving to make the next campaign in person, he caused very great levies to be made, set out on the 3rd of May, N. S., arrived, the 10th, at Lerida, where he held a council of war, in which it was resolved to besiege Balaguera; but the waters being out, and having advice of the re-enforcement his competitor had received from Italy, after he had invested the town, he judged it proper to draw off from before it, and return to Lerida. King Charles being informed of this march, privately raised his camp, and marched with such expedition, that having passed the Neguera, with the greater part of the army, at noon, on the 27th of July, he marched to meet the enemy, who immediately drew up on the rising ground of Almenara with forty squadrons, which were all their horse, and eight or ten battalions, while the rest of their foot advanced.

On another rising ground, which commanded that where the enemy was posted, the allies mounted fourteen pieces of cannon; and without staying for the right wing, charged the Spaniards so briskly with sixteen squadrons, that they broke and drove them upon their foot that were in the bottom, whom they trod down, and caused so great a confusion, that throwing away their arms, and leaving their baggage, tents, and a number of cannon and waggons, they fled by the favour of the night, which was coming on, to Lerida. King Philip arrived there at midnight, very much displeased with the behaviour of his horse. On his arrival, he was blooded, having been thrown by his horse, frightened with a cannon-ball, in the engagement.

After this victory, which cost the allies but four hundred men, they took in Balbastro, Estadilla, Sarizena, Guesqua, Abastello, and Moncon; all the garrisons of which places were made prisoners of war: and a great part of the kingdom of Aragon, as far as Huesca, submitted to King Charles, who, decamping from Moncon on the 12th of August, endeavoured to bring the enemy to a second battle. He passed the Ebro near Ozera, on the 19th, and marched directly to them; who, commanded by the Marquis de Bay, were posted on the rising ground of Jariexo, stretching the left towards Saragossa; he had the Ebro behind him, and the little River Huebra covered his front; each army preparing on the 19th of August, at night, for a general engagement the next day.

The Spanish cannon began to play on the very dawn, and made a terrible fire on the allies, who notwithstanding, marched up in order of battle, as well as the ground would allow, and receiving with surprising intrepidity the enemy's fire, began the attack at eleven o'clock. The generals, Amezaga and Mahoni, repulsed the left wing of the allies, and pursued them as far as Alagon and the Ebro, which advantage gave the Spaniards great hopes of the victory: but General Staremberg, charging, in his turn, the left wing of the enemy, and taking them at the same time in flank with a part of his foot posted behind hedges, they threw themselves in disorder on the main body, which they put into confusion, and caused an entire defeat of their whole army, about four in the afternoon.

King Charles, who had the satisfaction of supping that night in the tent of his competitor, took sixty-two colours and standards, twenty-two pieces of cannon, all the equipages, six thousand private men, and four hundred officers. General Mahoni, who, with some of the runaways, had thrown himself into the castle of Alfaxerea near Saragossa, was summoned, and having no hopes of succour, obliged to surrender prisoner of war with those who had followed him.

After this defeat, Philip, with an escort of two hundred officers, took the road of Madrid, where he arrived on the 24th. He immediately ordered money and provisions to be sent to his scattered troops, and drew five thousand men from the frontiers of Andalusia, to re-enforce his army, which was drawing together. In the interim, Saragossa, capital of Aragon, submitted to King Charles, and sent him a present of seventy thousand pieces of eight, with a quantity of clothing, ammunition, and provision for his army. After this the allies marched to Madrid: on their approach, Philip, not thinking himself secure, sent the rich furniture of the palace to Valladolid, which he the next day followed, with the queen, the Prince of Asturia, and all the privy-council and *grandees* of the court. He passed by the way of Montejo de la Vega, the ancient seat of the kings of Castile, and arrived the 16th at Valladolid, having promised the Castilians, by a letter, to return to Madrid in the space of a month.

This promise, however, did not prevent the town's submitting to King Charles: General Stanhope having summoned it on the 21st, four deputies were sent to Alcala de Henares; after which a general amnesty was proclaimed, and public rejoicings continued for three days. The allies having taken out of the church of our Lady d'Atocha, the colours they had formerly lost, encamped at Canillejas; and King Charles took his quarters in the stately seat of Count Aguilar, a league distant from Madrid. On the 28th, he made his entry into that metropolis, preceded by Count Galves's regiment, and followed by his guards, he marched through the streets of Alcala and Callemajor, to the gate of Guadalaxara, and from thence through the great square to our Lady d'Atocha, where he heard mass. He left the town the same night, without taking a view of the royal palace.

The promise Philip had made the Castilians to return to Madrid in a month, he made good; for the troops he had drawn together from all quarters formed so considerable an army, that the allies were obliged to quit that town on the 11th of November, and to withdraw to Toledo, which had submitted to King Charles. Philip, who returned to Madrid the 3rd of December, with Duke Vendome and the privy-counsellors, &c. who followed him, set out three days after, to place himself at the head of his forces. His design was to follow the allies in their retreat to Aragon, and bring them to a battle, in which, in all likelihood, he would have had the advantage, they being divided into several corps, that they might more easily subsist.

On advice that General Stanhope was at Brihuega, with eight battalions, and as many squadrons, he ordered it to be immediately invested. The cannon having opened a breach, the troops made the assault, and pushed to the very centre of the town, and, after a defence of twenty-eight hours, compelled this numerous corps to surrender prisoners of war; but on this condition, however, that the officers should not be spoiled of their equipages and horses. General Staremberg hearing the danger that Stanhope was in, marched with all the army to his succour, and in the night fired several cannon to give him notice of his arrival. On the 10th, he advanced as far as the plain of Villa Viciosa, whither the Spanish army, after the expedition of Brihuega, marched in order of battle to meet him, they being greatly superior in number.

The Duke of Vendome with the right wing, attacked the left of the allies, which he overthrew in an instant; then taking their horse in flank, routed them, and drove the foot, who maintained the fight till night, when they fled towards Seguenca, leaving behind them their cannon and wounded men, with a great number of waggons. The Germans give a quite different account, and say that the main body and right wing, consisting of thirty squadrons and sixteen battalions, were five different times attacked, and not only at length entirely defeated the enemy's horse, but drove the whole army of the Spaniards beyond the Tajune; killed six thousand, and remained masters of the field and all the cannon till noon of the next day. But this is not at all likely, for it is certain that this battle fixed Philip in that throne, the possession of which was the ground of this bloody war. But to return to the Low Countries.

Prince Eugene and the Duke of Marlborough arriving at the army on the 20th of April 1710, N. S., decamped that very night, to seize on the bridge at Vendin, and the upper grounds of Courieres. The French no sooner saw the vanguard of the allies, but they quitted their lines, which covered Walloon-Flanders, and which had cost them so much raising; so that the Duke of Wirtemberg and Lieutenant-General Cadogan entered them, without so much as drawing a sword. On the other hand, Monsieur d'Artagnon, who was posted behind the Scarpe, with forty battalions and thirty squadrons, not only abandoned the river the very next day, but also the four towers, Marchiennes, Hanon, and St. Amand, threw some troops into Bouchain, and withdrew under the cannon of Arras.

This successful opening of the campaign, was followed by the siege of Douay, invested the 23rd. This town, in which Philip the second, King of Spain, founded a university in 1560, was taken by Lewis XIV. in 1667, five days after the trenches were opened, since when that monarch had it regularly fortified, and raised a fort on the Scarpe half a quarter of a league distant from the town. We opened the trenches in two places on the north side of the river, the 3rd of May at night. While we carried on our works, Marshal Villars, having re-enforced his army with all the men he could draw out of the garrisons, gave out that he would march to the succour of the town; and in effect appeared with his army between Lens and Taupou; he even made a detachment, which, advancing as far as Neuvirel and Berticourt, drew very near to the lines we had made before the grand army, to prevent being incommoded during the siege, as we had been at Lisle. These motions raised the hopes of the besieged, and animated them to a vigorous defence; but all their bravery could not save the place, which capitulated the 25th of June; the garrison, four days after, gave the allies possession of that and Fort Scarpe, and marched out with all the marks of honour, to be conducted to Cambray.

The Partisan du Moulin attempted to surprise Lovain, but was disappointed by the bravery of the *burghers*. On the 6th of August he detached a party, who scaled the wall between the old and new gate of Brussels, where the ditch is dry, and having the good fortune to enter the town without being perceived, disarmed the *burghers'* guard, opened a gate, and let in their comrades to the number of four or five hundred; who posting themselves in St. James's churchyard, sent a party thence to the heart of the town, who seized upon the guild, and secured the *burghers'* grand guard.

After this expedition, they intended to possess themselves of the other gates; the garrison, which was but a hundred and fifty men, having withdrawn, on the first notice, into the castle. In the interim, the whole town was alarmed, and the *burgher*-master awaking with the noise made in the streets, ran disguised to St. Peter's Church, where he shut himself in and rang the alarum bell. Immediately the *burghers* took to their arms, and, headed by Van de Ven, marched to the square, and drew up in order before the guard. Du Moulin hearing that all was in motion, sent in all speed an officer on horseback, to see how matters went. He came to the square with his drawn sword in his hand, and threatened the *burghers* to fire the town, if they did not lay down their arms: but this menace was so far from having the desired effect, that one of them fired at him, and the ball taking him in the throat, tumbled him dead from his horse.

The *burgher*-master immediately ordered the inhabitants to repair from their different quarters to the gate the enemy had opened, and retake it; while he, at the head of his company, marched with beat of drum to St. James's churchyard to dislodge the French. But they, fearing they should be cut off from the gate, thought of nothing but their retreat; and it was time for them to do it, for the *burghers* arrived just as they left the churchyard, and hooted them as they went off.

In our march to the siege of Douay, one Morgan Jones stole from me one of my mares, and I was obliged to purchase another, which I did of a hussar, who, as I apprehended, had stolen it from a boor. This latter found her in my possession, though I had docked, trimmed, and endeavoured to disguise her; but to no purpose, the peasant was not to be deceived; he knew and claimed his beast. I denied her to be his property, as I had bought and paid for her; and told him I would not part with my right; I talked big, and thought to carry it off with a high hand; but the fellow complaining to Lord Orrery, and making oath the mare was his, I was ordered by his lordship to return the man his beast, at night, when we were come to our journey's end, which I accordingly did, but could never get my money back from the hussar. Soon after, a friend of mine, found where the Welchman had sold my mare, which I recovered; and my husband meeting Morgan Jones, gave him a sound drubbing for his thieving.

After the reduction of Douay, the allies encamped with the right near the head of the Lave, and the left near that of Souchet, behind the Scarpe, whence a detachment of twenty-six battalions and eighteen squadrons was detached to invest Bethune, on the 6th of July; and on the 22nd, Baron Fagel and Count Schuitenburg opened the trenches, one on the side of St. Andrew's gate, and one before that of the Holy Ghost. The town was well furnished with everything necessary for the holding out a long siege; it was defended by deep ditches, a great number of mines, double outworks on the side of the low grounds; one would have thought it was out of danger, they being lain under water, had double outworks, and was on a stony soil.

The allies, however, found means to drain off the water on that side where the grounds were drowned, and having carried on their work without being molested by mines, preparations were made on the 28th to give the assault to the outworks; but the besieged, not daring to expose themselves to it, hung out a white ensign. At Count Schuitenburg's attack, Baron Fagel resenting the governor's not doing the like on his side, continued to push on his works; and thinking his honour at stake, threatened, in case they longer delayed to do it, to lay all in ashes. Monsieur de Vauban, who commanded in the town, made some difficulty of this, because, as he alleged, there was no breach as yet on the side of the baron's attack; however, he was at length obliged to give way. The capitulation was signed, the garrison left the town on the 30th, with all the marks of honour, and was conducted to Arras.

As ours was one of the regiments which covered the siege, I had no occasion to run into danger. Captain Montgomery, who would serve volunteer at this siege, was killed by a musket-ball; and while it continued, all our foragers had like to have been cut off: Marshal Villars had detached several squadrons to attack us, which fell on those that were to protect us, and soon made them give way; but our foragers making head, and sustaining them, the tables were turned in our favour, and we drove the enemy with great slaughter: fresh troops coming to their assistance, we were compelled to retreat to a village, where we expected succour from our army.

We were soon surrounded, and summoned by the French to surrender, but we refusing, they attacked us in front, but in their turn obliged to retreat at the approach of the piquet-guard. In this excursion for forage, I got out of a barn a large bolster full of wheat, two pots of butter, and a great quantity of apples, all which I carried safe to my tent. The wheat I got ground at a mill the enemy had deserted, and made pies, which I sold in the camp: of the bran I made starch.

After the reduction of Bethune, as soon as the works were filled up, and the breaches hastily repaired, or rather botched up, the Prince of Orange, *stadtholder* of Frise, invested St.Venant on the 4th of September, with twenty battalions; as on the same day the Prince d'Anhalt-Dessau, with forty battalions, did Aire. Monsieur de Guebriant, who commanded in the latter, made all the necessary preparations for a vigorous defence. The drains we were obliged to make at St.Venant to carry off the water, were a great hindrance to the siege, for the trenches were not opened till the 16th, at nine at night, between the road to Busne and that to Robec, by two thousand workmen, supported by four battalions; and, nine days after, our batteries began to play.

We gave several assaults to the outworks, and almost carried them on the 28th, at night, and as the besieged saw we were going to raise batteries to play on the body of the town, they capitulated on the 29th, and were allowed to march out with all the marks of honour. Our regiment, I mean that to which my husband belonged, marched with the prince to the siege; and the English being commanded to attack the counterscarp, my husband, who was unjustly forced to do another man's duty, being in the front rank, firing on his knee, received a musket-ball in his thigh: I was just then got into the rear of those who attacked, being willing to get as near to my husband as possible, when I saw his comrades bring him off; I was greatly troubled, but felt nothing like the grief which seized me when I found my dear Richard Welsh among the dead; I knew nothing more dangerous for him than to catch cold, as it was commonly fatal, wherefore I stripped off my clothes to my stays and under-petticoat to cover him up warm, and his comrades carried him to the trench, where Mr.White the surgeon, who searched and dressed his wound, said it was but slight, but the next day, finding the bone broken, judged it mortal.

When St.Venant had surrendered, our wounded men: were carried to the army at Aire, before which town the Prince d'Anhalt-Dessau opened the trenches in two places on the 12th of September, at night. One on the left of the hornwork adjoining to. the gate of Arras, against the bastion of St. Stephen's gate; and the other before the old castle, on the side of the village of St. Quentin. The stony ground, the great rains we had this autumn, and the brave defiance the besieged made, contributed to the length and difficulty of this siege. The garrison disputed the ground inch by inch, and behaved with exemplary courage; the allies, however, surmounted all these obstacles; they at length threw bridges over the first ditch for the fifth time, for the garrison had burnt the bridges no less than four times; carried the covered way in the beginning of November, filled up the ditch which led to the breach, and having prepared the last batteries, compelled the garrison to beat the chamade on the 8th, between five and six in the evening.

The next morning the governor waited on the Duke of Marlborough to draw up the articles; at night he gave up to the allies one of the gates of the town and Fort St. Francis, and on the 11th the garrison marched out with four pieces of cannon, two mortars, and all the marks of honour. This siege put a period to the campaign, we were ordered into winter-quarters, and our wounded men sent to the hospital at Lisle, where my husband daily grew worse, had his wound often laid open; but at length it turned to a mortification, and in ten weeks' time after he received it, carried him off.

As in this town I had no acquaintance, I had no business. Brigadier Preston was the only one I knew, and he from a pure motive of generosity allowed me a crown a week, and a dinner every Tuesday, if I ought not to attribute this goodness to a grateful remembrance of the care I took of him when he was lain up with a wound he received at Ramillies. Over and above this, whenever he had any entertainment, I was allowed, for my assisting the cook, to carry away with me victuals sufficient for three or four days' support.

The unanimity of the allies was the principal cause of a successful war; but now the divisions, which were revived in England between the Whigs and Tories, paved the way to, and at last concluded, a less advantageous peace than might have been expected from such a number of conquests, and so many glorious victories.

About the 8th of April, N. S., the Emperor Joseph was attacked with a violent distemper, which in spite of all the advice of his physicians, daily increased; and no wonder, since they at length discovered that the remedies they had prescribed, were contrary to the nature of his malady, which proved to be the smallpox. However he was not thought in danger till the 15th; but the next day his imperial majesty complained of a great heat in his bowels, and a great heaviness and distraction in his head. This, augmenting the consternation the court was in, caused so great disputes among the physicians, that they passed the whole night in disputes, and came to no conclusion till the morning, when the emperor was past taking any remedy, and he had but life enough to receive the sacraments; after which the *nunico* having given him the apostolical benediction, he gave up the ghost at ten o'clock, in his palace at Vienna, in the thirty-third year of his age.

The Grand Army was early drawn together at Orchies, where it remained till the 30th of April, N. S., and from thence marched on the side of the plain of Douay, without entering upon anything of importance, on account of the French giving out that they would send a large body of troops into Germany, under the command of the elector of Bavaria, to take advantage of the consternation caused by the death of the emperor; but these designs proved abortive, by the allies having the precaution to send a very considerable detachment to the Upper Rhine. Though nothing of consequence was undertaken on either side, after we had taken post between Valenciennes and Douay, we had two or three skirmishes with the enemy; and on the arrival of Prince Eugene, marched to Lens, to give the French a fair opportunity to come to a general battle; they made a show of being inclined to it, by laying bridges over the Scheld, and altering the situation of their army, though they had no such intention: however, seven or eight hundred of our men were ordered to force a fortified post at Arleux, whom I followed, in the piquet-guard, sent to support them, in case they should be succoured by the French.

Our detachment carried the post, made several prisoners, and began to fortify themselves strongly in it, a large body of troops being sent to cover them. These the French surprised in the night, and put into disorder; but those whom they were to cover, awaking, and falling on in their shirts, sword in hand, the others rallied, and the enemy was repulsed. The next morning, going into the wood near our small camp, I found a hussar's horse tied to a tree with a tent upon his back as good as new; the horse, though but a low one, was very handsome, and mighty fleet: I suppose the owner, who was one of the enemy who attacked us in the night, had not time to lead him off. The French, after our removal, retook this post.

During this time of inaction, (for I account such bickerings hardly worth notice,) the Prince of Orange, who had shown me so great humanity in my affliction for the death of my first husband, quitted the army to make a tour to the Hague, to terminate the difference between his highness and the King of Prussia, with regard to the inheritance of King William's estates. He left us on the 11th of July, N. S., but to my great sorrow for the loss of my generous benefactor, he was drowned at Moerdyk on the 14th, being about twenty-four years of age; his body was found on the 22nd by a boat of Bergopzoom.

A few days after this fatal accident, the general of the allies gave out that they would attack, on the side of Arras, the lines the French had drawn to cover the country of Artois, behind which they had hitherto lain. In effect, the Duke of Marlborough, having advanced as far as Villers-Brulin, which was but two leagues from those lines, ordered the horse to cut several thousand fascines to fill up the ditch; and on the 31st of July, N. S., sent the heavy baggage to La Basse, under the conduct of general Hompesch, that he might have no encumbrance.

This detachment, which seemed designed for nothing more than an escort, being joined by part of the garrisons of Douay, Lisle, and Saint Amand, and being increased to eight thousand foot and two thousand horse, General Hompesch, their commander, directed his march with all the expedition possible towards Arleux, and Bac a Bacheul, to pass there the River Senset, from which the Marshal Villars had withdrawn his forces to strengthen his army, believing he should be attacked in his lines: but the allies, who had only amused him, precipitately decamping on the 4th of August, N. S., at night, and dividing themselves into four columns, marched by the way of Nouville and Talu straight to Vitry, where they crossed the Scarpe, and from thence towards Arleux and Bac a Bacheul to support count Hompesch, who was already there. The Duke of Marlborough, that he might get thither soon enough, went before, with all the horse of the right wing. Marshal Villars could scarce believe the first intelligence he received of this march; but having advice by which he was convinced, he also raised his camp.

However, as the allies were too far before him, and it was not possible for him to overtake them with his whole army, he placed himself at the head of twenty squadrons, to dispute them the passage of Senset. But having crossed a defile near Marquiou, he found count Hompesch drawn up in order of battle on the other side the river, supported by the Duke of Marlborough at the head of the horse. The good countenance they showed prevented his taking advantage of the distance of the rest of the army, which did not get, till night, as far as Oisy, and made him determine on a retreat. The crossing the Senset rendered the French lines useless, for it gave the allies an entrance into the enemy's country, without the loss of a man, and was looked upon as a masterstroke of the Duke of Marlborough. The first consequence of this expedition was the siege of Bouchain, which, on the 12th, baron Fagel invested with thirty battalions and twelve squadrons.

Marshal Villars, to impede the siege, and keep a communication with the town, raised an intrenchment near Marquette, which was extended as far as the morass of Bouchain, and in it posted twenty battalions: the besiegers, notwithstanding this, undertook to close their circumvallation on that side, and carried it from the rising ground to the morass between the enemy's intrenchment and the town, and at length, by extending it across the morass by making firm ground, with pontons, fascines, and blinds, quite finished it. This having rendered the marshal's endeavours fruitless, on the 23rd, at night, three trenches were opened, one against the lower, the other two against the upper town.

On the 30th, about half an hour past seven, our batteries began to play, and made such a terrible fire the subsequent days, that the garrison, not being able to stand, made but feeble opposition to our approaches, so that on the 11th of September we were masters of the half-moon at the attack of the lower town, and the breaches were made at the two other attacks; which obliged the governor to capitulate at two in the afternoon next day; but as he was refused all composition, the parley was broken off, and the attack renewed: however, about midnight, he again ordered the chamade to be beat; consented to surrender prisoners of war, and soon after delivered up a gate to the besiegers. The garrison, which made, still, three thousand men, marched out on the 14th, and were conducted, taking the road of Marchiennes, to be carried by water to Ghent and Sas van Ghent. Our army entered on no other expedition this campaign.

During this siege I was constantly employed in my Lord Stair's, kitchen under his cook, into which Colonel K——— coming, would have been rude enough, if I had not disengaged myself with a case-knife, just as Lord Forrester came in, who asked what was the matter, I told him the colonel was but a bad judge of mankind, who were to be read by their actions; had he considered that the love I bore my husband had brought me in search of him for many years, in a red coat, exposed to all the dangers and hardships of a soldier's life, he would not have made an attempt so unbecoming his character, and so little probable of succeeding. The colonel said he only intended to kiss me.

My lord commended and rewarded my virtue with a piece of gold, while he gave the colonel a gentle and friendly reprimand, who, poor gentleman, a few days after, had his heel taken off by a musket-ball, which wound laid him up for a considerable time. As I was one day a marauding near the besieged town, I got a basket full of fowls and pigeons, which I presented to the wounded colonel, to whom I was reconciled, as he had begged my pardon; these were no trifling matters, considering the French army and ours were so near each other that there was hardly subsistence for both; to which I may add the danger of stirring abroad, when a number of the enemy's parties were always in motion. The colonel took this present in so good part, that he gave me three barrels of strong beer he had in his quarters, and has been ever since very generous to me, which I cannot say of a great many others, to whom I had been much more serviceable.

Nothing happened to me in particular all this campaign of 1711, which was the last the Duke of Marlborough made, to the no small regret of the whole army, by whom he was entirely beloved, not only for his courage and conduct, but equally dear to us all for his affability and humanity.

During the siege of Bouchain, Charles III., king of Spain, was elected emperor, of whose affairs, with relation to the Spanish monarchy, the succession to which was the principal ground of the war, it will not be amiss to take a short view. After Philip had won the victory of Villa Viciosa last year, 1710, he once more became master of the whole kingdom of Aragon, the subjects of which were obliged to renew their oaths of allegiance to him. This reduction being made, the duke of Noailles at the head of fifty squadrons and forty battalions, invested Gironne on the 16th of December; he opened the trench before the Red Fort, and having carried it, attacked the town on the same side.

On the 13th of January, N. S., two breaches were of a sufficient width: but on that day there fell such a violent rain, that it drowned most of their works, and the tar, overflowing, undermined and overthrew their batteries, laying all the adjacent grounds under water; which reduced the besiegers to great straits, as it hindered their going to the barns, which served them for magazines. When the rain ceased, they began to repair the damage; the miners renewed their labour, and on the morning of the 24th they sprang a mine, which had all the effect they could desire; and the besiegers mounting the breach sword in hand, carried the first intrenchment, and were preparing to attack the second, when Count Tellenbach, governor of the town, sent to the Duke of Noailles to capitulate. The garrison had their liberty granted, and the French entered the town on the 26th.

After the rendition of Gironne the troops went into winter-quarters; Philip chose Saragossa, to be at hand to give his orders; he made great preparations, and new levies, giving out that they were designed for the siege of Barcelona. In the interim, Count Staremberg having received from England large remittances of money, and some troops from Italy, which increased his army to thirty-six battalions and forty-four squadrons, opportunely possessed himself of Pratz del Rey, a very advantageous post, from which all the endeavours of the enemy could not remove him. Wherefore, while the two armies were disputing the ground, the Duke of Vendome, that he might lose no time, detached Count Muret with three thousand men, whom he soon after re-enforced with the like number, to form the siege of Cardona.

This town could hardly be said to be fortified; but it had a good castle, and a numerous garrison. It was invested on the 14th of November. The old towers were soon demolished by the enemy's cannon; and on the 17th, in the morning, the besiegers having made an assault, carried the rampart, entered the town, made a cruel slaughter, and obliged such of the inhabitants as had not withdrawn into the castle, to surrender prisoners of war. Being masters of the town, they turned all their strength against the castle, the garrison of which, having hopes of succour, employed all possible means for their defence. They were reduced to the eating their horses and asses, when Count Staremberg sent a detachment, which on the 21st of December, being advanced within half a league of the castle, drove the besiegers, and vigorously repelled twelve companies of grenadiers, which attacked them near the spring of Aqua Rosa, to dislodge them.

The rest of that day and the next were employed in keeping the enemy in motion to gain a passage for four hundred men, laden with provisions, into the castle; which was luckily effected, by the besiegers abandoning their post on the approach of the troops, which sustained the convoy: they, however, very strenuously endeavoured to gain the rising ground, which the allies had in possession, but all their efforts were ineffectual; and after having lost two thousand men, killed or taken, they thought fit to retreat, and carry off what baggage they could: they left, notwithstanding, in their camp, fourteen pieces of cannon, four field-pieces, four mortars, a number of mules, with a good store of provision and baggage. This loss made the Duke of Vendome take the advantage of the night and a great fog to decamp from Pratz del Rey.

The allies never had so numerous an army in Flanders, as this year; and the Duke of Ormond, who succeeded the Duke of Marlborough in the command of our forces, in passing through the Hague, protested he would exert himself to bring the French to listen to reason. Notwithstanding which, when a fair opportunity offered, and a resolution was taken to attack them, he declared he had no orders to act against the French. The other generals were quite enraged to see the enemy escape such an evident danger. However, they could not think of remaining inactive the whole campaign with so fine an army, and notwithstanding the Duke of Ormond refused to employ any part of our forces in the siege of Quesnoy, that town was invested by the rest of the allies on the 8th of June, with twenty squadrons and thirty battalions under the command of General Fagel. Though in that season there is very little light, and the moon was then at full, these inconveniences did not prevent the opening the trenches, two before the ponds, on the right and left of the wood, and a third on the 23rd, at night, to divide the forces of the besieged. The town would have capitulated on the 3rd of July, but they could get no better terms than to be made prisoners of war.

New instructions were sent to the Duke of Ormond; in consequence of which, he withdrew from the rest of the army, encamped at Avene-le-sec, with all our English troops, consisting of twenty battalions and nineteen squadrons, and proclaimed a suspension of arms at the head of our camp.

To the end the allies might be rendered incapable to undertake anything considerable against France, the duke of Ormond endeavoured to draw off the German troops in English pay, and to bring them to enter into the suspension of arms; with this design, he gave them advice of his going off, and summoned them to follow him: but they refusing to obey, except only one battalion and four squadrons of Holstiens, and two of Walef, he sent the same orders again to the Prince d'Anhalt-Dessau, general of the Prussian troops. This prince returned for answer, that he had received one from the king his master, with command to obey the English general in whatever should not be contrary to his instructions, by which he was enjoined to act offensively as well as defensively; and if he received contrary orders, the king commanded him to withdraw, and join his forces to Prince Eugene's army.

The Prince of Hesse-Cassel, also summoned to follow us, thus addressed himself to the officer who carried him the order: Sir, tell the duke of Ormond that the Hessian troops desire nothing more ardently than to march, provided it be to engage the French: I will do myself the honour to acquaint His Excellency with the reason I cannot now obey his orders. The army decamping from Haspre on the 15th of July, to march to Thian, the Danish, Prussian, Saxon, &c. troops in English pay, left us and joined Prince Eugene. Though the withdrawing our forces considerably weakened the army, the allies undertook the siege of Landrecy, which the Prince d'Anhalt-Dessau, with thirty-five battalions and thirty squadrons, invested on the 17th.

When we decamped, the Duke of Ormond made a feint of taking the Ypres road, and of staying in that neighbourhood; but soon changed his route, and made an expeditious march towards Ghent and Bruges, which two places he surprised and garrisoned; and thus became master of the pass of those convoys, which the allies received by the Lis and Scheld.

On the 19th of July, France gave possession of Dunkirk to the troops the queen sent thither from England.

I left the allies before Landrecy; who, to keep open a communication with Douay, Tournay, and Marchiennes, had posted eleven imperial regiments and six battalions in an intrenchment at Denain on the Scheld. Marshal Villars being informed very minutely of the strength and disposition of the allies, and consequently of the corps at Denain, as it was given out, by the Duke of Ormond, resolved to surprise these troops. After several false motions to deceive the allies, and to make them believe he intended to succour Landrecy, he on a sudden changed his route, and being re-enforced by the garrisons of Cambray and Valenciennes, on the 24th of July, he with his whole army furiously fell upon the little camp at Denain.

It was impossible for the Earl of Albemarle, who commanded this body, to withstand the whole French army, or even to retreat, as we had taken away the most convenient bridges. Wherefore, after a short but very sharp engagement, the intrenchment was carried, and all who defended it, officers and soldiers, were killed in the action. The next day, the victorious French appeared before Marchiennes, but a weak town, which they took with little trouble, though it was defended by seven or eight battalions under the command of Brigadier Berkhoffer. Here they found not only all the artillery and ammunition designed for the siege of Landrecy, but all the provisions, brought together at a prodigious expense, for the support of the army.

The court of France, on the advice of this success, no longer doubted of the allies being compelled to accept of such conditions of peace as the English and French had prescribed them: they were confirmed in this opinion by the taking a hundred and fifty *barks* laden with ammunition and provisions, not to reckon the other booty the French made; the raising the siege of Landrecy, and the retreat of the allies towards Mons. In effect, those losses had so greatly weakened the confederates, that far from being in a condition to undertake any enterprise, they were not able to prevent Marshal Villars retaking several towns this campaign. The marshal being flushed with his turn of fortune, re-enforced his army, by draughts from several garrisons; invested Douay on the 3rd of August, and on the 4th, at night, opened the trenches before the town, and before Fort de la Scarpe. He left the care of the siege to Marshal Montesquieu and Count Albergotti, while he himself, with the grand army, observed the motions of Prince Eugene; who, after the raising the siege of Landrecy, had retired, and advanced very near to Tournay to succour the besieged, did he find it feasible. He encamped at Seelin, extending his right towards Noailles, and his left as far as Mons en Pevele.

After he had been several times to reconnoitre the enemy's lines, it was thought too dangerous an attempt to attack them: however, the prince spread a report, that the army would march to the relief of the town, and actually they decamped and drew near to the enemy; but as this motion was made with no other view than to encourage the besieged, the army soon returned to its post. General Hompesch, who had thrown himself into the town, with some troops, before it was invested, defended himself with all the bravery that could be expected with a weak and an ill-provided garrison. He held out till the 10th of September, and was allowed no other conditions than that of surrendering prisoners of war.

Before the end of this siege, and after Prince Eugene's retreat, Marshal Villars marched towards Valenciennes; and on the 8th of September, having led his troops over the Scheld, he advanced to the plain of Sebourg, to deprive the allies of all communication with Quesnoy; and that he might entirely cut it off, he threw up an intrenchment behind the little River d'Hanneau, by which, having straitened the town, he invested it in form. On the 18th he opened the trenches in three several places; at the gate of Valenciennes, at that of Cambray, and between these two gates: some days after, he opened another before the gate of the wood, that he might divide the fire of the besieged. General Ivoy commanded in the town, which they had scarcely had time to fortify; the governor defended himself with all imaginable bravery; but the French, notwithstanding, carrying on their works with the utmost vigour, made themselves masters of the outworks without great loss; and having made a breach, filled up the ditch and finished the galleries, all the grenadiers of the army were commanded to prepare for a general assault on the 4th of October.

Before it was given, the marshal summoned the governor, who not being strong enough to withstand the enemy, beat the chamade about four in the afternoon, and was obliged to undergo the same fate with the garrison of Douay. Towards the end of the siege of Quesnoy, the chevalier Luxemburg invested Bouchain, having first driven all the cattle in the neighbourhood, part of which he sent to Cambray; and opened the trenches the very day that Quesnoy surrendered. The town was attacked with such resolution, that, having but five hundred men in garrison, these were obliged to surrender on the 20th. The garrison left the place the next day, and was conducted to Chateau Cambresis, and from thence to Rheims.

In the midst of these disasters, the garrison of Ostend gained a considerable advantage over the French. Monsieur Caris, governor of that town, being informed of the weak condition of the garrison of Fort Knoque, sent the partisan La Rue, with, a hundred and fourscore men, who, by by-ways, got thither on the 4th of October, at night. There were four houses between the drawbridge and the fort; in these they found means to conceal themselves, and, at the gate opening, seized upon the two nearest bridges, surprised the guard, possessed themselves of the other gates, and disarmed the garrison. This was the last expedition of the campaign in 1712.

Sometime after our troops had taken possession of Dunkirk, I applied to his grace the Duke of Ormond, for a pass to England; which he not only signed, but generously ordered Major M——y to give me money enough to defray my charges; though he gave me but ten shillings, which I am satisfied was much less than the duke designed me; for everyone, whether friends or enemies to his grace, will allow he was not close-fisted. I left Ghent, and went by water to Dunkirk, where I was kindly received by our regiment, garrisoned in this town. As I was obliged to wait here some time for the packet-boat's arrival, I went to pay my respects to the governor, General Hill, to have my pass signed: he was then very ill and confined to his bed. He, however, signed it, sent me two *pistoles*, and a compliment, that had he not been ill he would have seen me; directing orders to be given to the commander of the packet, to respect me as an officer's widow.

During my stay here, I was going to take potluck with Colonel Ingram, and accidentally meeting him in the way, I told him I designed to foul a plate with him; said he, 'I should be glad if you would defer the favour to another day, as a set of officers are invited to dine with Brigadier Durel, and it is probable, that beside a better dinner, you may get wherewithal to defray your charges to England'

I thanked him for the hint, and took his advice, but they had dined before I got thither. Durel seeing by my looks I was disappointed, asked me if I would take up with a morsel at the servants' table. 'O my consience,' said I, 'you have shown the height of good breeding, to sit down before I came, for I don't suppose but Ingram had acquainted the company that I intended them the honour of mine; however, my pride shall never defraud my belly, and I don't know but I go into the politer company of the two; for had they known, as you did, that a person of my distinction would condescend to grace their table, they would show the good manners you have wanted, and wait my coming.'

They all laughed at the gravity with which I delivered myself, and I left them to get my dinner, reprimanding Durel for his want of respect to a lady of my rank and figure. Having eat heartily, and very much at my ease, I returned to, and took a cheerful bottle with the company, the Brigadiers Durel, Godfrey, Clayton, Sir Robert Monroe, and Colonel Harrison. One of the company was in a fine laced suit, of which, taking more than ordinary care, raised a desire in the rest to have them spoiled: they, to that end, plied him well with wine, never let the bottle standstill, but pushed it round, in hopes he would either spill the wine upon his clothes, or stain them with a second flask; but the care of them increased as he grew drunk, and they were disappointed of their aim: this made them propose the mischief to me, and as I loved a little roguery as well as the best of them, I pretended I could not finish my bottle.

The company, except the gentleman in the fine clothes, who was heartily in for it, seemed willing to excuse me; but he, who sat next me, swore I should take my glass in my turn: the more reluctance I showed, the more strenuously he insisted upon my pledging him every time the glass came round; at length I told him, if he forced me to drink when it went against my stomach, I might, however unwillingly, be offensive to the company, and particularly to himself and Brigadier Godfrey, between whom I sat. All arguments were vain, as commonly they are with drunken people, (and he was far from being sober,)— drink I should, let the consequence be never so fatal. I was very sober, but willing to gratify the rest of the company, and show the brigadier the effects of obstinacy, which are commonly loss and disgrace, took my glass, and prepared to cast.

At the third glass, after the dispute, I again desired him to excuse me, for I found another bumper would overcharge me. He was deaf to all I could urge; drink it I must, and drink it I did, to his great mortification; for I set open a flood-gate, which falling like a cataract, spread ruin and desolation over one side of his clothes; the colour of which changed to a dismal hue, and all the glory of the glittering lace sunk oppressed by an inundation of indigested wine. A pallid ire now o'er-spread his cheeks, and indignation sparkled in his eyes, while fetid fumes arising from the flood, forced him to strip, and at a distance hurl the now-polluted robe.

But to quit my heroics; however angry he was, he did all he could to conceal it, as he thought he alone was in fault, for he had not the least notion of his misfortune being designed. His clothes he could wear no more till that side was taken off, and a new one supplied. However, though he supposed it a mischance, and not premeditated, he could not forget or forbear telling me of it every time he saw me afterwards; but I excused myself by throwing the blame on him. I pretended to be very sick and fuddled, and was for taking my leave, but the gentlemen would not part with me till they had contributed to the charges of my voyage, giving me two crowns apiece.

Soon after, I embarked for England, and being arrived, took lodgings at the Queen's Head, Charing-Cross; having rested myself three or four days, I waited on the Duke of Marlborough; in my way to his grace's house met Colonel Chidley, and told him to whom I was going, and what was my errand, which my reader may suppose was to get some provision made for me, in consideration of my own service and the loss of two husbands in Her Majesty's. The colonel told me that he was afraid the duke had no interest; however, advised me to go, as I did, and was very humanely received by his grace, who expressed a concern that he could not serve me, and gave me a gentle reprimand for not coming to England when he sent, and had the power to do for me. Indeed his grace was so very generous to send for me, before he resigned his command, which I forgot to mention in its proper place. I returned my lord duke thanks for the good intentions he had, and took my leave; at going away, he clapped a guinea in my hand, and honoured me with his good wishes.

My hopes being here frustrated, I was resolved to try if I might have any better success with my lord Duke of Argyle, who was still in the enjoyment of his sovereign's favour. Accordingly, the next day, I set out for his grace's house, but near King-street, Westminster, I met him in his chair. The duke first espied me, and asking a footman of his, to whom I was perfectly well known, whether that was not Mother Ross? being answered in the affirmative, stopped his chair. He asked me several questions, how long I had been in England, &c., and lastly, where I lodged? I answered him, that 'it was in one of your houses of civil conversation, more frequented than any one in Flanders, and more noted for the modest company and conversation to be found there;' which was the reason that the officer of the parish, who represented Her Majesty, very often did my landlady the honour of his visits, and not seldom invited the ladies under her tuition to a palace of his, known by the name of the Round-house. His grace smiled, and giving me a guinea, bid me go to his house, and wait his return, saying he would consider how something might be done to provide for me; bid me inquire for Macquin, who with Sawney Ross, were the only two of the duke's domestics to whom I was known.

According to my orders, I inquired for the former of these two, and was shown into the housekeeper's room, who went up to her lady, and told her that I was in the house. Her grace, having had my character from her lord, sent for me to her apartment; made me sit down; breakfast with her, and tell the story of my adventures: which I did, in the best manner I could; and though I was as concise as possible, I believe I omitted no material event that regarded me in particular. Her grace was so complaisant as to appear pleased with the account I gave, and I am sure was very much so when I related his grace's escape at Rousselart, telling me, for that advice which I gave her lord of the enemy's approach, she should always esteem me, and do me any service I could ask that was in her power, and remember me to her latest hour; and indeed her grace kept her word, for she heaped many favours on me, which I mention in honour to her conjugal affection for her lord, and with true sense of the many obligations her humane goodness has lain me under.

When I had finished my story, my lady duchess made me a present of a guinea and a half, enjoining me silence, lest it might prevent her lord from making me any. I had scarce made an end of my narrative, when his grace came in, and finding us together, was very merry with her grace receiving in her bedchamber, and conversing with, a dragoon. When dinner was ready, my lord duke would have done me the honour of seating me at his table; but as there was company, I begged to be excused, and with much entreaty was permitted to dine at the second, from whence, after our meal was over, my lord sent for me to the company, with whom I sate till evening.

My lady duchess, who saw me under some restraint, and at a loss how to behave before a person of her character and quality, soon left us; in getting off her chair she kissed me, saying, I know you and my lord will be better company, and talk over your camp adventures with more freedom in my absence; but I desire you will let us see you often, and be better acquainted. Her grace judged very right; for on her retiring, we ripped up old stories, and were as merry as so many new-paid-off sailors. There were with my lord two of his *aids-de-camp*, who had as good memories as I had. When it grew dark, I took my leave, and my lord giving me another guinea, ordered me to get a petition drawn up for the queen; to carry it to the Duke of Hamilton, and he himself would back it. As I went off, the two *aids-de-camp* made me a present of three crowns each.

As his grace of Argyle had advised me, I got a petition drawn, in which was set forth that for twelve years I had served in the Earl of Orkney's regiment as a man; that I had received several wounds, and lost two husbands in the service. With this I waited on Duke Hamilton, who said, as he did not know me, I might possibly be an impostor; my bare assertion not being sufficient proof of my service. I replied, that I would appeal to any officer in the army, as I believed that I was known to all, though I did not know them all. His grace answering, he required no greater confirmation, went into a parlour, where I heard some discourse pass, but could distinguish nothing. After some little time I was ordered to go in to the duke, and found two officers of our regiment, with whom I was intimately acquainted. They saluted me with a great deal of good nature, and confirmed to the duke all that I had advanced in my petition, saying much more in my favour than modesty will allow me to insert here.

'Well,' said the duke, 'after having run through so many dangers together, you cannot but take a bottle at meeting.' His grace called for one, and, having emptied it, I took my leave; at going away the duke gave me a crown to have a new petition drawn to present to the queen myself next morning; he intending to present Her Majesty the other that night. I thanked his grace, and was very punctual in following his instructions. I got my petition finely written out, dressed myself the best I could, the next day, and went to court, where I did not stay long before her majesty came down the great stairs, (at the bottom of which I had planted myself,) led by the Duke of Argyle, who I suppose was talking of me, because Her Majesty eyed me very earnestly, and his grace often smiled upon me.

As soon as she came down, I fell on my right knee, as I had been instructed by the yeomen of the guard, and delivered my petition, which the queen was graciously pleased to receive with a smile, and helping me up, said. It should be her care to provide for me; and perceiving me with child, added, 'If you are delivered of a boy I will give him a commission as soon as he is born:' but to my sorrow, it proved a girl, who has caused me great trouble and vexation. Her majesty was further pleased to give me an order to the Earl of Oxford for fifty pounds, to defray the charge of my lying-in. I often waited on that noble lord, but could neither get money nor access, which I humbly represented to the queen, who gave me, in her great goodness, a second order for that sum to Sir William Windham, who paid it me without the trouble of going twice to receive it.

Sometime after I was brought to bed of the child I went with when I presented my petition to the queen, Lord Forrester and Lord Fofard ordered me to be at the King's Arms in Pall-mall, where they were to dine with some other noblemen and gentlemen of the army, designing to make a collection for my immediate support. I was punctual to the time their lordships had appointed; but none of the company being yet come, I waited at the door, with my child in my arms. While I was at my post, a soldier who had served abroad seeing me, very wisely concluded that I was a lewd woman, and began to treat me as such in the grossest language; and after a volley of G—d d—me's, mixed with the common flowers of rhetoric b—h and w—re, said, it was a burning shame the nobility should encourage a pack of idle lewd b———s, and support them and their b———ds with that bread which they ought rather to distribute among such as had ventured their lives, and spilled their blood in the service of their country; he concluded this friendly salutation with a blow of his stick across my breasts.

The language he had given me was provocation sufficient to inflame me; but a blow was an indignity never before put upon me, and enraged me to such a degree, that not considering I had the child in one arm, I flew upon him, and began to belabour him with my right fist. A drawer who saw the disadvantage I was under, took the child from me, and having both hands at liberty, I gave him such a thorough beating, that he cried out for quarter; but I, deaf to everything but resentment, rolled him in the kennel, and had demolished him if he had not promised to beg pardon in the most submissive manner, which indeed he did, alleging in defence of his insolence that he did not know me, but now that he was informed who I was, he was ready to acknowledge I deserved whatever was done for me, and would show me more respect for the future.

Out of evil, it is said, often comes good: this insult, and the consequential battle, proved very lucky to me, for it happened as the quality was returning from court, who stopped their chariots to be spectators of the fray, in which I received neither hurt nor loss, but that of my sarcenet hood being torn, which however was amply repaired by the money Lord Harvey and the Marquis of Winchester threw me out of the tavern window, and that I had from others of the nobility, which amounted to upwards of nine pounds, beside a large quantity of untouched provisions from the tables of such quality as dined at the King's Arms that day.

A few days after this, as I was sauntering in the Court of Requests, I met with two of my countrywomen who sold fruit, &c.: one of them, a single woman, named Judith, was my acquaintance in Ireland; the other, whose name was Mary, had only two husbands, one living in Ireland, and one in Drury-lane. This latter, as two of a trade can never agree, took it into her head to reflect on the reputation of the former, who, good-natured girl, always traded on her own bottom, whereas the other not only dealt on her own stock, but got money also by other folks' wares. As I was talking with Judith, I thought it a piece of impertinence, and an insult upon me, to attack her at that time, which I resented by giving her first a severe thrashing, and next, in a public manner, the discipline schoolmasters give their idle scholars, which afforded no small diversion to the spectators, especially to the gentlemen of the livery.

On a Saturday morning, the 15th of November, 1712, having some business at Kensington, as I went through Hyde Park, I saw four gentlemen jump over the ditch into the nursery, which made me suspect a duel, and hasten towards them to endeavour, if possible, to prevent mischief; but I could not get time enough, for they all four drew and engaged, two and two, with great animosity; one, who I found was Colonel Hamilton, instantly closed in and disarmed his antagonist, General Macartney, and at the same time the other two fell, the one upon the other. These were Lord Mohun, and the Duke of Hamilton; the former fell dead upon the spot, and the latter expired soon after. Colonel Hamilton was wounded in the instep, and Macartney, as some keepers came up, walked off, and was not taken; though a reward of several hundred pounds was offered for the apprehending him.

Had I been examined as a witness in this affair, my affidavit might, possibly, have left no doubt; but it was very happy for me I was not thought of, as my evidence would in all probability have made enemies of my friends; having often experienced the charity of several noblemen, intimates of the deceased lords, and I must have disobliged one side, as I should have sworn to the truth of what my eyes had witnessed: which, as it is not now material, I shall not declare, but refer my readers to the history of those times.

It was not long after this, that, instigated by a strong desire to see my friends and native country, which I had not visited for some years, my circumstances being very easy by the queen's bounty, and the charitable assistance of the nobility, and officers of the army, I wrote to my mother to let her know I would be in Dublin in a short time, and indeed got there before her, who, though upwards of a hundred years of age, travelled ten miles on foot to give me the meeting. The poor old woman, who had long given me over for dead, having in so many years heard nothing from or of me, wept for joy, and in such an excessive manner, when she embraced me, that I could not refrain mingling my tears with hers, my transport being equally as great.

Upon inquiry after my children, I learned that the elder of them died at the age of eighteen, and that the younger was in the workhouse. The nurse, with whom, at my departure, I had left the best of my goods, together with my child, soon threw him upon the parish: her tenderness for my poor infant being measured by her interest, she was soon tired of the burden he was to her. Indeed, but one of those with whom I had intrusted my effects, was honest enough to give me any account of them, and that was Mr. Howell, father to the person who ruined my virgin innocence; all the others, like the nurse, thought the possession I had given them warranted their converting my goods to their own. use, and looked upon me as an unreasonable woman to expect a return.

My misfortune was, that the honest man had but few, and those the worst of my goods, which he kept safe, and restored justly. I had no better luck with regard to my house; for the person whom I left in it, when I went to Holland, dying, one Bennet set up a claim to it as his freehold, and got possession, there being none in my absence to contest his title, and I could not out him, as my writings were lost or destroyed: and indeed what could I have done had I had those evidences? I had not money sufficient to carry me through a lawsuit, and to expect justice without money, is much the same as to think of reducing a fortified town without ammunition: I was therefore compelled to sit down by my loss, and think on some method to get an honest living.

As I had before kept a public house, and was used to sutling in the army, I could thing on nothing better than that of my former; and accordingly, I took a house, put in a stock of beer, and by this and making pies I got a comfortable support, till my evil genius entangled me in a third marriage with a soldier named Davies. He had served in the First regiment of Foot Guards in the Low Countries, but on the conclusion of the peace between France and the high allies, he was, at his own request, discharged from the service. His father dying during his absence, and leaving him a small patrimony, he left Flanders and went to his brother, who lived near Chester, to take possession of the provision his father had made for him; but his brother, who had lain hold of it, and knew he was not in circumstances to compel him to do justice, made a jest of his pretensions, and to this day keeps to himself what their father had designed for his support.

This unexpected disappointment obliged him to betake himself, once more, to a military life, and coming over to Dublin, he was enrolled in the Welch Fusiliers. After my marriage with this man, I continued on my public business, till his regiment was ordered to Hereford, in the first year of King George I., when a weak effort was made in favour of the Pretender. I stayed behind him in Dublin no longer than was absolutely necessary to dispose of my effects; which having done, I got a pass from the secretary of war, and followed my husband to Hereford; from thence I went to Gloucester, designing for London, where I intended to settle.

The Jacobites being somewhat elated, some who were in the commission were little cautious in declaring their sentiments, and I met with a good deal' of trouble with regard to the signing my pass, and also with the under officers, who were disaffected to the Hanover succession; but the favour and contributions of His Majesty's loyal subjects make me ample amends. At Colebrook I met Colonel Floyer, with whom I supped, and the next day, pursuing my journey, I arrived in London. While I was travelling to town, my husband was on his march to Preston, where the rebels were assembled.

Her late Majesty, beside her bounty of fifty pounds, had ordered me a shilling a day subsistence for life, which the Lord-Treasurer Oxford, without the queen's knowledge, reduced to five-pence. The ministry being now changed, I flattered myself that I should have justice done me, and be restored to my whole allowance of a shilling: with these hopes, I addressed myself to Mr. Craigs, who produced the warrant, and generously undertaking my affair, got the king's order for my receiving the shilling as intended by Queen Anne, which I have ever since enjoyed. I lost a good friend at the death of this gentleman.

By the time the Preston rebellion was quelled, I had settled myself in a house in the Willow-walk, Tothill-fields, Westminster, where I took to making farthing pies and selling strong liquors, and had such success that I was soon able to purchase, at a large expense, a discharge for my husband, which was just so much money thrown away; for in two days after his arrival in town, being in drink, he enlisted in the guards.

One night after my husband was in bed, and I in a manner undressed, some frolicsome sparks, thinking they show a great deal of humour in being sillily mischievous, took it into their heads to tear up the pitching-place which I had made for porters to ease themselves by resting their burdens upon, and to throw that and the board on which I exposed my pies into the ditch; no doubt they would have done further mischief had I not run down, followed by my husband and a lodger, all three almost naked, and put a stop to their career. I gave the worthy gentleman whom I first laid hold on, such a thorough rib-roasting, that he was glad to cry quarter, and to promise that he would make good the damage, and give us a treat for the pains we had taken to convince them, by weighty arguments, that the pitching-place and pie-board were more convenient where I had set them, than where they had thrown them.

The house I lived in, and two adjoining, I rented of —— S——ley, esq., at eight pounds a year. I repaired these, and bought the willows before them of a former tenant, by whom they had been planted. My landlord, notwithstanding, being in distress of money, let my tenements over my head to one Bilby a bailiff, on a long lease, for the sake of a fine, which the said Bilby paid him; without giving me the least intimation. The Sunday after the lease was signed, Bilby let me know that for the future I was to pay my rent to him, that he thought the tenements under-let, and I must either agree to the raising my rent next quarter, or provide myself elsewhere.

I used all the rhetoric I was capable of to divert him from so great cruelty, as I termed the raising my rent; but finding he had no bowels, and that entreaties and submission only flattered his pride and made him more obdurate, as is the nature of these low-bred upstarts, who are purse-proud, I resolved to vent my passion, which with much difficulty I had hitherto curbed, and changing my dialect, I treated him with all the opprobrious terms I could think of; and though I say it myself, there are very few, if any, of the academy of Billingsgate, was a greater proficient in the piscatory salutations. I hope my readers will not attribute this to me as a piece of vanity, when they reflect that quite through this long account of myself, I have all along guarded against that weakness, and only related pure matters of fact.

The next day, my new landlord brought a carpenter with him to lop my trees; I foreseeing this would be the ground of a quarrel, secured my husband, that he might not have an assault sworn against him by Bilby, and went out myself with a resolution, if possible, to provoke him to strike me first, and in such case, to belabour him to some purpose. The carpenter was got into a tree, and Bilby stood below to secure the branches as they fell; but I forced them from him, and upon his asking the reason, told him the trees were my property, that I had bought and paid for them to such a one; he replying that he was a rogue, I readily acknowledged that he might very well be called so, with respect to honest men, but with regard to a bailiff, and especially to so vile a cannibal as he was, the man ought to be allowed honest. Bilby, irritated at the compliment, endeavoured to wrest the branch I had taken, out of my hand, and finding he struggled in vain, he gave me a blow.

I never received one before with pleasure; but I own the stroke afforded me a particular satisfaction, as it gave me an opportunity to pommel the rascal with impunity, and I did not let it slip; for I flew at him and beat him unmercifully, as I was greatly superior to him in strength. The carpenter, seeing his comrade to roughly handled, came down to his assistance, and, endeavouring to take me off him, tore my headclothes, which was directly quenching fire with oil; for I left the bailiff, who took that opportunity to make a precipitate retreat, and leave us to fight it out. I, having seized the carpenter, struck up his heels, and falling upon him with my knee in his stomach, I let him rise, but it was to knock him down again, which I did till I was quite spent with thrashing him and forced to give over, though much later than the poor fellow could have wished; for he often endeavoured to get clear of me, and follow the example of his principal, which he did as soon as he could, and wed he had better heels than hands.

About this time there was a camp in Hyde Park, where I kept a sutler's tent; Lord Cadogan, when the king came to review the forces, treated his majesty and the prince, with a great many of the nobility, and was so good as to send for me to stand sentinel at the tent door; but to my misfortune, having nobody I could trust with my business, my husband being to perform exercise in the foot guards, I could not do that duty. However, I resolved at all events to see the king; but finding several general officers in a tent joining to that in which his majesty dined, I stepped in to them without design of staying; but they plied me so well with strong-bodied wines, that I had almost forgot what I went upon; they gave me a shilling apiece for a kiss, which I gave them, and went to see the king: but I had delayed too long, His Majesty was going into his coach when I came up; however I got so near, that he perceived me, and with great humanity said, he thought to have seen the old dragoon sooner.

I prayed God to go with His Majesty, and he drove off, leaving me disappointed in my expectations. I went to take a view of the pavilion which was formerly taken by Prince Eugene from the Grand Vizier in Hungary, and certainly the richest I ever saw. While I was looking upon this magnificent piece of work, I remembered that the nobility who attended on his majesty and the prince, were entertained in an adjoining tent; I immediately went thither, and was admitted. I acquainted them that I had lost several pounds in the camp, by scoring their followers, and hoped they would take it into consideration.

On this one proposed contributing a guinea apiece, which was so great and seasonable a relief, that without it I must either have perished, or gone upon the parish; for the fatigue of cooking, and the effect which the loss of the money I trusted in the camp, had on my mind, threw me into a tertian ague, which compelled me to leave the camp the following day. As to any assistance from my husband, it would have been the highest of folly to have expected it, as he always spent more than he got; nay, so inconsiderate was he, that the day after I left the camp, he sold my tent and everything in it for forty shillings, though the tent alone cost me fifty; and, notwithstanding the condition I was in, spent every penny of the money.

While I was lain up with the ague, I heard the news of the Duke of Marlborough's death; which additional trouble, for I was greatly indebted to his grace's goodness, both abroad and at home, increased my illness, and even to this day affects me; he had been my colonel, general, and benefactor, and the remembrance of what I owe to his humanity, will make me lament his death to the day of my own. I was, at the time of his funeral, well enough to go abroad, though very weak; however, I went to the late duke's house, and, placing myself by my husband, marched in the funeral procession, with a heavy heart and streaming eyes. When the ceremony was over, I left the regiment in the camp, and returned to my house.

When I was thoroughly recovered, unwilling to be troubled with my landlord Mr. S——y and his new tenant the bailiff, I settled at Windsor: the former ot these, being overwhelmed with debt, and threatened with a gaol, put an end to the menaces of his creditors and his own life by cutting the veins of his wrist; the latter met with a just reward of his rogueries.

I lived a private life in my new settlement, supported by the benevolence of the nobility and gentry to whom I had the honour of being known; and which was much more considerable than at present, as many of my benefactors are dead, as some imagining that what they gave me was extravagantly thrown away, and others, that I got considerably elsewhere, have either curtailed, or quite withdrawn their former charity; so that, at this day, I have not one-third of the benefactors I then had.

Having spent a whole year at Windsor, I grew tired of so inactive a life, and resolved to get once more into business. I removed to Paddington, took a public house, and by my diligence, and complaisance to my customers, had their number daily increase. Here, as elsewhere, I continued my visits to such as honoured me with their protection, and to whose generous contributions I was indebted for greater part of my support ever since my arrival from Flanders.

Among the rest of my benefactors, there was a noble lady who made me several presents, and one day gave me a hoop-petticoat, a machine I knew not how to manage; and no wonder, for I never had one on before, and I believe it requires as much dexterity to exercise as a musket; however I was resolved, since it came at such an easy rate, to show away in it, and accordingly, wanting something of a brazier, I put on my hoop, which made me fancy myself in a go-cart, used for children when they begin first to feel their legs. I could not help laughing at the figure I made; but my finery, which at my setting out was the subject of my mirth, occasioned me, before I returned, both pain and confusion.

In Knave's-acre, the footpath being narrow, I thrust against a post, which made the other side of my hoop fly up. I, who had never been hooped before, imagined it was some rude fellow thrusting his hands up my coats, and thinking slily to revenge the insult, threw my stick back without looking behind me, and gave my left hand, I carried on my wound, which has been always open, such a blow, that I could not help crying out. I turned about, but could see nobody but some apprentices, who came about me at my roaring, and set up a loud laughter at the awkward management of my hoop, which I heartily cursed, with its inventor, and made off, vexed and ashamed at becoming the sport of boys.

Soon after this, I was sent for by some men of quality, and gentlemen of distinction, who, for their diversion, had invited Sir James Baker, called by them Lord Lateran, to the Thatched House to dinner; to which, however, they sat down without his lordship, and despatched in a hurry, and ordering a couple of ducks, some beefsteaks, and soup, to be set by for him, went into another room, whither I was conducted, and taught my cue.

This Lord Lateran was a person with whose simplicity several of the quality diverted themselves; he was by some esteemed a fool, others thought him mad, and others again believed he wore a mask, and rather suffered himself to be laughed at and made the jest of the company, than go without a dinner; which must have been the case, had he wanted the sense to conceal that, he could not but have, of the tricks put upon him.

Soon after the quality with whom the mock lord was to have dined were withdrawn, as I have said, his lordship came in, and resented their not staying for him, as the highest indignity offered to a man of his quality. The drawer endeavoured to appease him by a detail of what was set by for his lordship. Hearing there was soup, of which he was a great lover, and an immoderate eater, he was somewhat pacified, ordered it in, and fell to, very heartily, a waiter attending his lordship's further orders. I, by the time he was seated, went up and knocked at the door; the servant, who had his instructions, opened it, and asked my business; I asked if Sir James Baker was there.

'Madam,' said the waiter, 'I know no such person, there is nobody here but my Lord Lateran.'

In the interim, the devisers of this plot on the poor lord, slipped in, and concealed themselves behind a screen that was between him and the door.

The fellow naming Lord Lateran, I answered, he was the very person after whom I inquired; went abruptly into the room, and seated myself opposite to him. His lordship seemed both confused and nettled at this freedom; he stared at me, and when he had recovered his surprise, asked what my business was, whence I came, and who sent me thither, desiring I would be expeditious, as he was but just set down to dinner.

'My dear,' said I, 'I do not design to interrupt you in your meal, as I came on purpose to dine with you, though this pretended ignorance of me causes both my grief and astonishment, since you cannot but know that I had more regard to your solicitations than to my interest, having entirely disobliged all my friends by becoming your wife.'

'Wife! Wife!' replied my lord in amaze. 'Why woman I never was married!'

'Is it possible, my lord, a man of your quality and good sense can bring a blemish on his honour, by denying what he is conscious can be so easily proved? It is happy for me and my two babies, as like you as one pea to another, that I have three witnesses of our marriage, or I find you would ruin my character and bastardize your poor innocent children.'

'Children too! very fine truly, I have a wife and two children without knowing anything of the matter!'

'Lookye, my lord, I am not a woman to be trifled with; your simple denial will avail you nothing against the oaths of three credible, nay, creditable witnesses, though it has given me such a contempt for your person, that I can part with you and not break my heart; but I expect you will, and that immediately, furnish me money for my and your children's support.'

'Why, thou thoroughpaced impostor! thou notorious abominable liar!'

'Go on, my lord; money I must and will have; this mean foul language is a scandal to your quality, but does not affect me or make me less your wife.'

'So I find you will swear I am married, to extort money out of me.'— His lordship then turning to the drawer, who, though an actor in the farce, kept his countenance, which was naturally austere, desired he would do him the favour to hand that gentlewoman downstairs, and set his foot in her b——h.

The fellow, prompted from behind the screen, answered, that he durst not part man and wife, as he did not know how dangerous it might be with regard to the law, extremely severe in such cases. My lord, in a fright, asked him if he thought I was really his wife; 'As God is my judge,' said he, 'I never was married to her.'

'I cannot tell that,' replied the other; 'She avers, and you deny it; she has witnesses to prove it upon oath, and you cannot prove a negative, let her evidence appear.'

'There is no occasion for that,' replied his lordship; 'this is some abandoned battered old jade, who can no longer get money by whoring, and would now extort it by swearing a sham marriage upon me: I don't question her being prepared with false witnesses.'

'Come, my dear lord,' said I, 'fall to your soup, and after dinner, I will show your ingratitude by giving incontestable proof of our marriage.'

As his lordship was pretty sharp set, he took my advice, and fell to very heartily, protesting it was the best soup he had ever eat, only a little too salt. He had reason to say so, for the wag of a cook had pissed in it, and for that reason had bid me eat none. When his lordship had finished the soup, I bid the waiter bring me a plate, a knife, and a fork. 'Why sure,' said my lord, 'you don't intend to dine with me?'

'Indeed but I do, and bed with you too. Do you think I married to have only the bare name of a wife?'

'Prithee woman, be quiet; if you want a dinner, stay till I have done, or get to the sideboard. Was there ever such a vile impudent woman?'

'Was there ever such an unkind husband? but, my dear, you can't be in earnest, this is only to try my patience!'

'I protest, if I had my sword here, I would run you through the body.' He spoke this with such emotion, that he set our audience upon the titter, and had like to have discovered all. The steaks and ducks being set upon the table, I desired he would help me; but he was now grown sullen, and I could not wrest a word from, him; wherefore, without ceremony, I helped myself, where I best liked. Having dined, I told him I would now take my leave in hopes of finding him in better temper another time, but I entreated one kiss at parting.

'No, no, woman, I kiss you? Kiss the devil's dam.'

'I will have a kiss before I go.' Saying this, I got up, and made towards him; he endeavoured to avoid me, and I chased him round the room before I could fasten upon him, and when I did, I held him fast round the neck and kissed him spite of his resistance; this threw him into such a passion that he would have run out of the room, and infallibly have seen the company behind the screen, but I got hold of him and gave them an opportunity to get off. When I thought they were got off clear, I let my lord go, who made the best of his way down stairs: when at the bottom, he threatened the master of the house that he would ruin him, for suffering such an insolent jade to affront a man of his quality.

The company who set me to play this roll, were highly diverted with the performance on all hands; but, for my part, I can't but believe the mock lord smelt a rat, and was as little angry as I was fond. My reasons are, he eat heartily; could not but hear those behind the screen titter, and also hear them go out of the room; but it was his interest not to discover them. In short, they laughed at my lord, and my lord, if the truth was known, laughed at them. However, if I guess right, he carried on the jest, by industriously avoiding me if by chance he at any time saw me in the streets.

While I lived at Paddington I applied myself to some friends, who at my request got my husband's discharge from the foot-guards; but in this I wanted foresight, for he falling into his former extravagances, was so far from being of service to me in my business, as I had hoped he would, that I was obliged to throw up my house and shop, sell off my goods, and procure a pass from lord C—— t for Ireland. When I came from that nobleman's house, where I had been for the above purpose I passed by that of Lord S——x. Two of his footmen who were at the door, stopped me, and the gentleman ran to tell his lord that I was below. Upon the gentleman's returning, he told me that his lord wanted me to tease Sir James Baker, who with a great deal of company, was at table with his lordship. I was very glad of the opportunity, and followed the gentleman upstairs, who, pointing to a room, and making signs for me to go in, I rapped gently at the door, and somebody called out. 'Come in.'

I obeyed the order; several of the company, strangers to me and the story of the Thatched House, were, at my entrance, pretty much surprised; but more so, when they saw Lord S——x smile upon me. I put on a seeming confusion, and begged pardon for being so unmannerly as to intrude into a strange company in a nobleman's house, but hoped they would think me rather an object of their compassion than resentment, when they knew that it was the unkindness of a husband, for whom I had the tenderest affection, forced me to take a step, which I was sensible could hardly be excused by any other motive.

'My lord,' said I, 'my name is Baker, and as I heard Sir James Baker is in this company, I have taken the liberty to inquire after my husband.'

'Madam,' replied my lord, 'there is no such person here, possibly

139

you mean Lord Lateran; if it is that noble lord you seek, you have not lost your labour, he is at table.'

The moment Sir James heard me name him, he turned his head, and spying me, in a violent, if not a feigned, passion, vented himself in these or the like words; 'Thou wicked, vile, base, infamous woman, why dost thus haunt me?'

'How!' said my Lord S— x, 'by this language she cannot be your lady, for Lord Lateran has too much honour to treat a wife with such harsh language. Then turning to me, as if I was entirely unknown to him, he continued; 'Woman, look to what you are about, men of quality are not to be insulted with impunity; you must not think to impose on that noble lord; you call yourself his wife, if you do not prove it, I have a good pump in my yard to revenge the insult on that noble person, and may perhaps cure you of your vile practice.'

I desired his lordship not to judge partially or rashly, but that he would give me leave to speak. His lordship said it was just and reasonable to hear what I could offer. 'My lords,' said I, 'my simple assertion, I am sensible, would little avail me; but I have living witnesses of the truth of what I have advanced; witnesses, my lord, who were present when the priest performed the ceremony of our marriage, besides two sons, the fruits of it, enregistered in his name, and long acknowledged his children by himself It is true, that ten years since he left me, without any just matter of complaint against me; for I defy the world, censorious as it is, to cast the least reflection on my honour; my enemies allow me a woman of insuperable virtue.'

'Oh! the vile strumpet,' cried Sir James.

'Let her proceed,' said Lord S———x, 'she speaks with an air of truth, and your passion makes me fear there is some jealousy at the bottom of this affair.'

'Z———ds,' said Sir James, 'your lordship can't believe that infamous wretch; upon my honour I never saw her but once before, except in the streets, and then she pinned herself upon me at the Thatched House.'

'Let her go on,' replied Lord S———x.

Continued I, 'I am to this day ignorant of the reason why he left me, which, I must own, greatly afflicted me; for he was a very fond husband for the space of three years that we lived happily together.'

'Not three minutes, my lord, on my honour,' cried Sir James; 'the devil must have spirited up this incubus to persecute me.'

I went on; 'Your lordship cannot suppose that I have my witnesses always with me, wherefore, my lord, I put it upon this issue for the present, let him take his oath that I am not his wife; he dares not do it.'

Lord S——x said that would be descending below his dignity.

'Well, my lord, since he is now a man of quality, I am loath to expose him in a public court, and am ready to forget what is passed, if he will return with me to his own house. My dear Lord Lateran, you know how you have wronged me, but I will never mention the injury, all shall be buried in oblivion, and will seal this promise with a virtuous kiss.' I was going round to him, and he seeing no way to avoid me, leaped over the table, threw down some chairs, broke a few glasses, threw open the door, ran downstairs, threatening to kill the man who would stop him, and swore he would never more enter that house. In the streets he had all the actions of a madman, lifting his hands to heaven, doubling his fists, stamping; and as a footman who followed him, reported, threatening me with death.

When the laugh was over, which made some of the company hold their sides, and others wipe their eyes, Lord S——x ordered me to sit down, take a glass, and give the company my story; I obeyed his lordship, and was as succinct as possible. When I had finished my history, everyone at table made me a present of five shillings, and my Lord S——x bid me take a bottle of wine home with me.

Soon after this, having made money of my goods, I left Paddington and went to Charles-street, Westminster. Here having an order from the governors of Chelsea College to appear at the Board, as all do, at a certain time, who receive pensions as invalids, I went and made my appearance. In returning home through the Five-fields, I fell in with two pensioners, who had been on the same errand; one of them, who was an intimate acquaintance, stopped me to inquire after my health. His companion took an opportunity, from the difference of our pensions to abuse me, as undeserving that I enjoyed, having never done anything for the government.

Nettled at this treatment, I made a comparison between his and my service, greatly to my own advantage, and concluded with calling him a faggot and a cowardly dog. Stung with this appellation, he was resolved to show his bravery, for he drew, and made a thrust at me, who had no other weapon than my stick, with which I put by his pass, closed in with him, wrenched the sword out of his hand, threw it over the bank, fell upon him with my oaken plant, broke his head in two places, and belaboured him till he cried '*Peccavi*,' Two gentlemen, spectators of the fray, offered a me ten shilling treat, but my business would not let me accept it.

I now waited about the court that I might be in the way of my benefactors, and often received their benevolence, which enabled me to return to and settle in my native country. I took a house as near as possible to the castle, as I had great dependence on the Lord Lieutenant Lord C——t's family, and, indeed, his lordship's servants were the best customers I had, as my lord himself was my best friend, often giving me money to pay my rent, beside a privilege he allowed me, exclusive of all others to sell beer in the Deer Park on a review day; but, as there was a greater call for liquor than I could furbish, I gave a license to two others.

I stayed but one year in Ireland, which was as much owing to my inclination to rambling as to my business not answering my expectation; but while I was in Dublin, I happened one day to espy the Rev. Mr. Howell, who, as I have before shown, robbed me of my maiden treasure; he also had a sight of, and endeavoured to speak to me: I avoided him, and by turning into a coffee-house, eluded his design. He was now married, the father of eleven children, and settled in Shropshire, where my husband at this time was, He, finding that I carefully avoided giving him an opportunity to converse with me, went home to his brother's, where he lodged while in Dublin, and appeared very melancholy; every one inquired into the cause of his visible alteration; but his sister, alone could extort the secret from him. He told her that he had seen me, which brought fresh to his memory the injury he had done me, and the perjury he had been guilty of; that a reflection upon his injustice was intolerable, and gave him such pain, that he believed he should never recover his peace of mind.

His sister would have sent for me, but he would not suffer her; For, said he, I am sure she will not come, her resentment of the wrong I have done her is too strong. The next day he left Dublin, and about seven weeks after, his sister meeting me, read a letter, which gave her the melancholy account of his having destroyed himself. Change of kingdoms had made no change in his temper; his sadness daily increased, and he could find no ease, wherefore he resolved to put an end to his life, which was a torture to him: to this end, he one day rose very early, and went into his study; his wife, at her usual hour, got up, and preparing his breakfast, sent one of the children to give him notice that it was ready: the child, after having knocked several times at the door, without any one answering, opened the door, found him hanging in his sash, and quite dead.

At this sight the child screeched out, and fell into a swoon. The child's scream alarmed her mother, who, running up with some others of her children, saw the distracting sight; the poor woman was inconsolable, for she not only lost a husband she loved, but saw herself by that loss deprived of bread, with eleven children to maintain. Mr. Howell, some little time before he was guilty of this rash action, wrote a letter to his brother, in which he tells him, that the reflection on the injury he had done me, had robbed him of all peace of mind, and brought upon him such a settled melancholy, that he was in a state of despair, and bid him not to be surprised if he should hear that he had lain violent hands upon himself.

When I had resolved upon quitting Dublin, I sent a letter to my husband to take a house for me at Chester. Soon after he sent me an answer, and let me know he had taken a very convenient one for me in that town, and desired me to make all possible haste to get thither. On the receipt of this, I went to take my leave of Lord C——t, who, to divert himself, would needs see the ceremony of a camp marriage, so led Colonel P——t and me into the garden, where, laying two swords across, the colonel first and I next, jumped over them, his lordship performing the function of the priest, pronouncing the following words, 'Jump Rogue,—Follow Whore.' After the ceremony was over, my lord gave us a treat, and dismissing me, I went on board the yacht.

I met Colonel M——y and several land officers who were going to England in the same vessel. They asked if I had a pass, and I showed it them; but the captain of the yacht (whose surly temper and behaviour, and turning several poor people ashore who could not pay their passage, gave me a distaste) coming to me in a gruff manner, said, 'D—— ye where's your pass?' I answered him in as rough a style, and refused to let him see it. On this, he threatened to send me back, and I threatened to beat him, which was no small diversion to the officers, who egged me on to box him, but the captain had more wit. When we arrived at Chester, I showed him my pass, and, at the same time told him, I would acquaint His Majesty that he stole milliners' apprentices and made a bawdy-house of the king's vessel, which was true enough.

I lived three years in Chester, and then returned to Chelsea, where I have remained ever since, without anything happening worth notice. I got my husband into the college, where he is a sergeant, and have been hitherto subsisted by the benevolence of the quality and gentry of the court, whither I go twice a week; but the expense of coach hire, as both my lameness and age increase, for I cannot walk ten yards without help, is a terrible tax upon their charity, and at the same time, many of my friends going no longer to court, my former subsistence is greatly diminished from what it was.

LEONAUR

ALSO FROM LEONAUR
AVAILABLE IN SOFTCOVER OR HARDCOVER WITH DUST JACKET

THE WOMAN IN BATTLE *by Loreta Janeta Velazquez*—Soldier, Spy and Secret Service Agent for the Confederacy During the American Civil War.

BOOTS AND SADDLES *by Elizabeth B. Custer*—The experiences of General Custer's Wife on the Western Plains.

FANNIE BEERS' CIVIL WAR *by Fannie A. Beers*—A Confederate Lady's Experiences of Nursing During the Campaigns & Battles of the American Civil War.

LADY SALE'S AFGHANISTAN *by Florentia Sale*—An Indomitable Victorian Lady's Account of the Retreat from Kabul During the First Afghan War.

THE TWO WARS OF MRS DUBERLY *by Frances Isabella Duberly*—An Intrepid Victorian Lady's Experience of the Crimea and Indian Mutiny.

THE REBELLIOUS DUCHESS *by Paul F. S. Dermoncourt*—The Adventures of the Duchess of Berri and Her Attempt to Overthrow French Monarchy.

NURSE EDITH CAVELL *by William Thomson Hill & Jacqueline Van Til*—Two accounts of a Notable British Nurse of the First World War. The Martyrdom of Nurse Cavell by William Thompson Hill, With Edith Cavell by Jacqueline Van Til

NURSE AND SPY IN THE UNION ARMY *by Sarah Emma Evelyn Edmonds*—During the American Civil War

WIFE NO. 19 *by Ann Eliza Young*—The Life & Ordeals of a Mormon Woman-During the 19th Century

DIARY OF A NURSE IN SOUTH AFRICA *by Alice Bron*—With the Dutch-Belgian Red Cross During the Boer War

FIELD HOSPITAL AND FLYING COLUMN *by Violetta Thurstan*—With the Red Cross on the Western & Eastern Fronts During the First World War.

THE MEMSAHIB & THE MUTINY *by R. M. Coopland*—An English lady's ordeals in Gwalior and Agra duringthe Indian Mutiny 1857

MY CAPTIVITY AMONG THE SIOUX INDIANS *by Fanny Kelly*—The ordeal of a pioneer woman crossing the Western Plains in 1864

WITH MAXIMILIAN IN MEXICO *by Sara Yorke Stevenson*—A Lady's experience of the French Adventure

PERSONAL RECOLLECTIONS OF JOAN OF ARC *by Mark Twain*

LEONAUR

ALSO FROM LEONAUR
AVAILABLE IN SOFTCOVER OR HARDCOVER WITH DUST JACKET

A DIARY FROM DIXIE *by Mary Boykin Chesnut*—A Lady's Account of the Confederacy During the American Civil War

FOLLOWING THE DRUM *by Teresa Griffin Vielé*—A U. S. Infantry Officer's Wife on the Texas frontier in the Early 1850's

FOLLOWING THE GUIDON *by Elizabeth B. Custer*—The Experiences of General Custer's Wife with the U. S. 7th Cavalry.

LADIES OF LUCKNOW *by G. Harris & Adelaide Case*—The Experiences of Two British Women During the Indian Mutiny 1857. A Lady's Diary of the Siege of Lucknow by G. Harris, Day by Day at Lucknow by Adelaide Case

MARIE-LOUISE AND THE INVASION OF 1814 *by Imbert de Saint-Amand*—The Empress and the Fall of the First Empire

SAPPER DOROTHY *by Dorothy Lawrence*—The only English Woman Soldier in the Royal Engineers 51st Division, 79th Tunnelling Co. during the First World War

"TELL IT ALL" *by Fanny Stenhouse*—The Ordeals of a Woman Against Polygamy Within the Mormon Church During the 19th Century

FRIENDS AND FOES IN THE TRANSKEI *by Helen M. Prichard*—A Victorian lady's experience of Southern Africa during the 1870's

MEMOIRS OF SARAH DUCHESS OF MARLBOROUGH, AND OF THE COURT OF QUEEN ANNE VOLUMES 1 & 2 by A. T. Thomson

THE WHITE SLAVE MARKET *by Mrs. Archibald Mackirdy (Olive Christian Malvery) and William Nicholas Willis*—An Overview of the Traffic in Young Women at the Turn of the Nineteenth and Early Twentieth Centuries

MARY PORTER GAMEWELL AND THE SIEGE OF PEKING *by A. H. Tuttle*—An American Lady's Experiences of the Boxer Uprising, China 1900

VANISHING ARIZONA *by Martha Summerhayes*—A young wife of an officer of the U.S. 8th Infantry in Apacheria during the 1870's

THE RIFLEMAN'S WIFE *by Mrs. Fitz Maurice*—*The Experiences of an Officer's Wife and Chronicles of the Old 95th During the Napoleonic Wars*

THE OATMAN GIRLS *by Royal B. Stratton*—The Capture & Captivity of Two Young American Women in the 1850's by the Apache Indians

Lightning Source UK Ltd.
Milton Keynes UK
UKOW05f2027031213

222347UK00001B/99/P